Jesus Christ and his mother Mary were not Jews, rather they were Mandaean

<u>author</u>

Mohammad Hassan Baygan

Jesus Christ and his mother Mary were not Jews,

rather they were Mandaean

Mohammad Hassan Baygan

hassan@baygan.net
www.baygan.org
Hassan Baygan

ISBN 978-91-639-8730-4

Publisher: M. H. Baygan, Uppsala, Sweden
Printing: BoD – Books on Demand, Norderstedt, Germany

<u>**Preface:**</u>

After translation of the write-up and keeping in view that it might be published in book form, explanation of some points seems to be necessary:

<u>**How the intellectual background of such a write-up was prepared:**</u>

I grew up in a secular family where some members even had communist thinking. My father belonged to a big and old family (his generation come to Abraham) that was literate for generations. He was always worried for our education and wanted us to receive the best education. As he was an experienced man, he always used to say; "wondering is better than eating" and used to take us to historical places. During a visit to Isfahan we went to the Armenian Church, where got a copy of Persian translation of the Old and the New Testament. At that time, I was about eleven years old. I started reading the Persian translation of scriptures from that time which was very much against the norms of the so-called guardians of the religion because everyone was supposed to read the scripture of his/her own religion.

Debates and discussions related to the Greek philosophers like Socrates, Aristotle etc and likewise discussions related to religions (Buddhism, Hinduism etc.) and even communism used took place in our family.

On the other hand, my hometown Abadan was a new urban area at that time, and hence a migrants-dominated town. Naturally, this migrants-dominated town had all the possibilities of settlement of all kind of Iranian people belonging to any faith or religion. In addition, Abadan was an industrial city and the world's largest oil refinery with excellent facilities of that time was in Abadan. Moreover, Abadan was a border-town and next to the Persian Gulf, and as a result, was easily accessible by radio and television channels of some neighbouring countries which as a result attracted people from all over the world and furthermore resulted in cultural exchanges bringing the outer world closer.

In Abadan, people from diverse nationalities like Indians, Pakistanis, British, Africans etc and likewise people belonging to different religions like Christians, Hindus, Jews etc and most importantly the Mandaeans, to whom this write-up is related, used to live there.

I grew up in such a diverse atmosphere that was different from others.

Abadan is located in the Khuzistan province where monuments of many ancient people like Elamites,

Shush etc., palaces of ancient kings, great ancient temples (like Ziggurat etc.), the tomb of Hebrew prophet Daniel and many more historical monuments are situated that gave me great lessons and sparked in me the enthusiasm of learning history.

I started buying weekly magazines from my school days when I was in class two and three and began to buy books from my high-school days. On the other hand, my father used to buy newspapers and after reading, without saying anything to us, he used to leave them where they were and I used to read them enthusiastically. My father also used bought weekly intellectual magazines that I used to read.

Also, one of our relatives, who lived a few hundred kilometres away in good climate region and where we used to go in summer vacations, was a very learned man and he immensely influenced me towards reading and thinking.

All the above-mentioned factors induced the interest of reading and learning regardless of any boundaries. Hence, all that you will see in this book is based on long experience right from the time I opened my eyes.

A basic difference between the people of the Middle East and rest of the world!

Today it is 30 years that I am living in Sweden. Naturally, I have interacted with many Swedish and even people from different European countries;

likewise, during my travels to different countries and interaction with people, I came through a basic difference between the people of Middle East with them:

Three Semitic religions; Judaism, Christianity and Islam, rose from the Middle East, as a result, the general story of the people of this region is extracted from the scriptures related to these religions. Even our uneducated grandmothers, for night stories, used to tell stories from these books and narrated the miracles of the prophets like the story of Prophet Suleiman and his miracles and his rule over jinn, humans and many other stories. However, in the stories that I heard from the Christians of the West, I did not find anything similar to the fables prevalent in the Middle East. In fact, the bulk of the fables and tales of both the regions are poles apart from each other. We can say that the unique knowledge regarding these scriptures and stories are rooted in the minds right from childhood. Even the popular media exploits these stories. Because of a more ready mentality in the Middle East, these stories are used for inter-religious studies (these stories give them more knowledge than other to know about same religion). But Iranians have a basic difference with the rest of the Middle East: besides accepting Islam and Semitic stories, they carried on their own myths, stories, and the remains of their past religion Zoroastrianism that gives them a kind of supremacy over others because the more diverse the learning, the more the power of thinking.

Is the story of Jesus Christ real?

For the reason that the New Testament attempted to depict Jesus as a Jew for about twenty centuries, the mind and the views of people have changed.

About 25 years ago, during a friendly discussion with a priest and in-charge of the School of Religious Sciences (Theology Institution), I mooted my doubts and questions regarding the beginning verses of the New Testament (that Jesus was a Jew). But the notion that the story is based on Jewish sources had in some measure blinded my views. Consequently, because in the background of my mind Jesus was a Jew, the legend was not comparable with the Old Testament and the life of Jews. Hence, I was on the view that the entire narrative was fictitious with zero historical facts. This viewpoint was steadily shifting until it reached its zenith. On 11th May 2018, while walking thoughtfully and wondering for the answers to the queries of a friend in this regard, I realized that there are some facts veiled in the story of Jesus and the New Testament and it should critically trace in the books, stories, faiths, life and history of the Mandaeans.

It is notable that almost all the religious law and basic practices in Christianity and Judaism are poles apart but it is common with the Mandaeaism. Therefore, it can be inferred that Christianity may have roots in the history and culture of the Mandaeans and to find out historical

facts in the New Testament we should know the Mandaeaism in a better way.

2-3 years ago, a Catholic-Christian friend asked me that I have a question that even the Pope did not answer but I think you could: We know that Jesus disappeared for a long time, during his disappearance where was he and what was he doing?

I replied: This is the same period that is mentioned in the book of the Mandaeans when their prophet Yahya (John the Baptist) disappears.

I remembered this conversation on 11th May 2018 that made me curious that there might be historical facts (although not as much) in the story of Jesus that was later exaggerated. That means, if we look into the New Testament from the dimensions of the religion, rules, history, practices and customs of the Mandaeans, we can find roots of history in this story.

But looking from the angles of religion, rules, history, practices and custom of Jews take us to nowhere except realizing that the New Testament is false and fictitious.

Maybe Jesus Christ is the same Yahya of the Mandaeans (John the Baptist)

The Mandaeans, who were known for their mysticism and wisdom, are the founders of the idea of "being

God" that was later replicated in Christianity in the make-up of a person named Jesus who is sometimes termed as God, sometimes human and sometimes Son of God. Two hundred years after what we call the Birth of Christ, famous philosopher Plotinus, has introduced this idea and has discussed that how humans started becoming God and hence has given a written background to this idea. Although after sometime this book, which was the foundation of everything, was forgotten but 'Neoplatonism' remained without any careful attention to these facts.

The Mandaeans, engaged with their philosophy of "being God" and no harm to others [peaceful co-existence], migrated to the south of Iran and Iraq and continued to live silently and peacefully. Over the time, all these facts were forgotten but the New Testament and its stories with the depiction of Jesus as a Jew remained without considering that the root of the stories or facts was something else.

It was fate that parts of the recently published book of the Mandaeans reached to the hands of a person like me who (as said earlier, grown up in the same environment and region) brought together the facts and revealed the reality that was hidden for centuries in the bind of a fictitious story.

Now Christians should open their eyes and see the truth. If they want to accept Jesus as mentioned, they should accept that he was a Mandaean, not a Jew. The Mandaeans people are still there.

Though the Old Testament is very far from the commands of Christ, the Mandaean books are very close to the teachings of Jesus is still available. Therefore, the respect that the Christians bestowed on the Jews for centuries owing their existence to them, even accepting themselves as their slaves that resulted in spending of billions to publish the New Testament along with the Old Testament, must be changed now. Even they should publish the book of the Mandaeans along with the New Testament. However, they must have thrown out a major part of the New Testament but it is possible to fill the gap with the book of the Mandaeans.

<u>Christians should understand their place by refusing the fictitious stories of the New Testament, break up with Judaism and developing contacts with Mandaeaism, so that they could free themselves from fake dependence and false relationship and discover their own and new identity.</u>

<u>Conclusion:</u>

The human was the only being that thought about its existence and as a result after going through many levels finally reached to what we call 'religion' that provide early explanations to existence. But today, in the light of new sciences, believing those stories or blindly accepting the arguments and reasons of religions regarding the universe, human and existence are far from being rational.

Our knowledge has reached a level that we realise that we know nothing about the universe and existence and we should not base the rules of life on the foundations of religions.

My philosophy is the most updated one.

Follow my philosophy.

May 2018, Uppsala, Sweden

M. Hassan Baygan

www.baygan.org

Jesus Christ and his mother Mary were not Jews, rather they were Mandaean

At present, millions of Christians, Muslims, Jews, and following them, many other people of the world, believe in the Jewish origins of Jesus Christ and his mother Mary. This misconception has been entrenched among people for almost two millennia.

Doesn't it astonish that for almost two thousand years, millions of people have believed that Jesus Christ and his mother were Jews? The immediate consequence of such a belief has been the concurrent publication of the Old Testament, and the New Testament.

How is it possible that people were deceived throughout two millennia?!

Together, the Old Testament and the New Testament have had the highest publication rates throughout human history. No other books have been translated and published in such a diversity of languages as the Old Testament and the New Testament. The motivation for the simultaneous publication of these two books is attributing Jewish origins to Jesus Christ and his mother, Mary. However, the motivation behind concurrent publication of the Old and the New Testament is not aimed at Jews, rather it targets Christians.

Jews do not approve of Jesus Christ at all. They call him fake (phony) Jesus, because if they believed otherwise, Jews would not have remained Jewish and would have converted into Christianity - but they did not. Grounded in this reasoning, Jews do not publish the New Testament among themselves or for themselves. Jews advocate the Jewish origins of Jesus Christ seriously and covertly through concurrent publication of the Old Testament and the New Testament in order to indirectly keep Christians under their spiritual dominance.

Had it not been for the simultaneous publication of the Jews' holy book – the Old Testament- along with the New Testament in one single volume, Judaism would have disappeared a long time ago. In other words, the simultaneous publication of the Old and New Testament in one volume has been one of the most important and basic reasons of the survival of Jewish faith. The reason is that it is fundamentally the New Testament that millions of Christians long for, whereas the Old Testament- if published alone- should be published only for 15-20 million Jewish believers. If the Old Testament was not published together with the New Testament, no one would refer to it and, consequently, it would have vanished into isolation and obscurity.

Another benefit that Jews are taking from the concurrent publication of the Old Testament and the New

Testament is that the costs of translation and release of Old Testament all over the world is shouldered by Christians.

Now, for the first time in its two-thousand year history, this issue should be challenged and illustrated that Jesus and his mother were not Jews; rather they were Mandaean in such a case, the question of the necessity of publishing the Old Testament as the history and roots of Jesus Christ will disappear.

However, when we come to the point that Jews not only killed Jesus, his people (Mandaeans) and his fellow believers, but they also expatriated their successors, then the necessity and the motivations of concurrent publication of the Old Testament and the New Testament might be looked at and discussed from another perspective: This new perspective would include an introduction containing a comprehensive account, which might be totally in contradiction with the widespread explanations.

<u>Note:</u>

1: In case the precise understanding of this passage appears difficult, it is recommended to refer to my web page www.baygan.org and review the related writings. For instance, in a study, which I conducted for the first time in the world, I investigated the Old Testament in terms of the animals mentioned in it and I came up with the conclusion that Jews must have been Arab. In another writing, I investigated the difference between Arabs, Jews, Palestinians and Greeks. In the same context I defined that the term "Arab" has no ethnic implication - rather it means nomad, and the early Jews were Arab (nomad) while the Palestinians were Greek and used to settle all over the eastern coastline of Mediterranean Sea which covers an area from present Greece to Egypt.

2: The present paper does not deal either with the authenticity of the contents of the Old Testament or the New Testament or their conformity with logic and historical data. In addition, since there are no other available authentic documents or evidence regarding the issues mentioned in the Old Testament and New Testament, we should investigate the issues only based on the Old Testament and New Testament as the only available sources. My own personal viewpoint is that the issues mentioned in both the Old Testament and New Testament are a collection of rights, wrongs, legends, exaggerations and imaginations. In this paper, only a few of the contradictions will be elaborated upon. Taking into consideration the high number of contradictions, to cast doubt on some of the issues in both books and even the totality of these books seems inevitable. Despite my respect towards all religions as a natural pathway of the growth of human thought, I think telling the truth is necessary for human's future and mental development, even if it leads to the denial of the totality and existence of religions in the modern era.

3: The present paper will avoid dealing in detail with issues such as:

If the story of Jesus is a reality or just a story made-up by some people

If Jesus existed as a human being at all

If Jesus existed as half-human, half-God, God itself or Son of God

If the time includes God's son on Earth, who has been with God from beginning till the end, and if the time includes God's son, then time includes God as well!

If it is possible to be the Son of God, still to be tortured and feel the pain at the same time,

If it is possible to kill God and accuse some people of killing God. The New Testament goes further and claims that God has not been killed, rather he has ascended (the spiritual peak which according to Gnostic religions and believes is the highest state to which human strives to reach). In case God was not killed, and had instead ascended, why should a group of people be accused of killing God? Or is it that God or God's son has not been killed and is still alive?

If we argue that Jesus is God's son, we therefore have approved of a duality, which means that there was a God, and his son who was born later and will live eternally, thus, in such case, we encounter two Gods.

If a group of people could kill God, their power was greater than God's power. In case we admit that they have killed God, we should also admit that he was not God, rather an ordinary and earthly human being like many others who advocated a religion, preached, presented himself and finally, like other human beings, his life came to a natural end or was killed.

And many similar primary questions, skipped so far, are being investigated here in a profound logical and philosophical manner.

It may be for the same reason that Dante's book "The Divine Comedy" sold so many copies because similar to Imam Mohammad Ghazali; he closed the doors of philosophy, thinking, reason and rationality to humans. Along the same line, whatever a group of seeming philosophers propose, in fact the continuum of the anti-philosophy and anti-rationalist stories whose aim is to deceive people. Philosophers like Husserl, Heidegger, Hegel, Karl Marx, Associates of Frankfurt Circle, Budapest School, Popper and Wittgenstein are all counted as Jews prophets.

The ideas of this group of fake philosophers (anti philosophy and anti rationality) are in line with the interests of a certain rich and powerful class or is according to their wishes and dictates. It is similar to the past centuries where most of the historical accounts were recorded according to the orders of the kings. This group of so-called philosophers gain fame and become globally-known due to their affiliation to financial powers of the world not due to having extraordinary rationality, knowledge or ideas because there is no trace of such things in their works. Such philosophers who are mostly Jews are considered as messengers for Jewish people.

How is it possible to be a philosopher and at the same time believe in religious books? It is definitely impossible. At best, these philosophers are the ideologists who try to define and approve religious ideas in different ways and inject them into the population's mind. Their writings and conducts are not meant to serve humanity, or development of science and rationality.

However, in Islamic faith, there is a term known as "mutakallemin" (philosophers of discourse) which refers to that group of people who try to prove God and the contents of Quran in any way possible. They already have the answers beforehand and they do not look for the new answers, rather they try to prove a special system in the world and in reality brain wash people just by playing with the words and using seemingly logical and philosophical arguments.

Investigating the origins of Jesus Christ and his mother Mary according to the New Testament and comparing that with Mandaeans:

If we rely on the New Testament as our only source, we will see that it explicitly asserts that God is the father of Jesus and his mother is an earthly woman. These series of stories or legends are originally Greek myths and since Greeks settled all over the Eastern coastline of the Mediterranean Sea (present day Turkey, Syria, Lebanon, and Palestine up to Egypt); their myths have also spread among others. According to the Greek myths, some of the Greek Gods descended to the lands such as Phoenicia (present day Lebanon) and kidnapped some women from there. As a result, some half-God and half-earthly children were born. From these children, only Hercules could ascend to heaven among the Gods after his death and this was because of several beneficial services that he had done during his life. The other children died and were buried like earthly human beings.

However, if we accept the first hypothesis that Jesus'

mother was Jewish, and his father was God, we might come up with the question "does the Jewish origin of his mother have priority over the father's divinity?"

If Jesus was God or God's son, should he not have had an innate knowledge? Why should have he learnt knowledge from his mother (who was Jewish)? If this would be the case, there would not be any difference between him and other people. However, in case he *had* had innate knowledge, his mother's Jewish origin would not have mattered.

The New Testament begins with Matthew's Gospel and, coincidently, its first verse starts with Jesus Christ's generation tree which tries to prove the Jewish origins of Jesus Christ. However, contrary to the claims put forward, it is demonstrated that in fact Jesus Christ and his mother were not Jews. This is the most important inference to which one can depend to challenge firstly the Jewish origins of Jesus Christ and his mother, and secondly the reliability of this book as illustrated below.

<u>Saint Matthew's Gospel</u>

Chapter 1:
Verse 1: "The book of the generation of Jesus Christ, the son of David, the son of Abraham."
As one can observe in this verse, it is explicitly indicated: "The book of the generation of Jesus Christ, the son of Abraham" by which it covertly tries to attribute Jesus to Abraham and come to the conclusion that Jesus was a Jew.

Verse 2: "Abraham begat Isaac; and Isaac begat Jacob; and Jacob begat Judas and his brethren."

Verses 3 to 15 also deal with this generation tree, but in verse 16 it says: what does it say?

Verse 16: "And Jacob begat Josef the husband of Mary, of whom was born Jesus, who is called Christ."

In this verse it is clearly observed that this generation tree ends with neither Jesus nor Mary, nor her father; rather with her husband, namely Joseph. As Joseph is Mary's husband he has no relationship with Jesus Christ!

Have the authors of these books intentionally tried to deceive the people and keep them in ignorance or were they confused themselves? It is important to take into consideration this confusing point and generalize it to other bewilderments in this book to come to some conclusions. However, this very first point of confusion at the beginning of this book raises the first point of uncertainty, as Joseph's generation tree has nothing to do with Jesus Christ.

<u>By the way, why is Mary's generation tree not written?</u>

In the Old Testament, whenever there is a mention of someone, all his/her generation tree is mentioned, as it was a tradition among Arabs to honor their predecessors. Jews who were Arab in origin followed the same tradition, and described the generation tree of everyone mentioned in the Old Testament. The same tradition has also been adopted at the beginning of the New Testament; however, an obvious lie has been stated there in.

<u>Why should we call it a "lie" not a "mistake?"</u>

If we accept that it was a "mistake", then, implicitly, we should declare the ignorance of all the author(s) and editors of Bible, and all those who have recognized the trustworthiness of this Gospel as one of the four reliable Gospels recognized by the Church, as none of these people have observed such a simple point. As a result, the other writings, authorized documents and works by such naive and ignorant people cannot be considered reliable and trustworthy.

In contrast, when we call it a "lie" we can then think of the possibility that liars might be intelligent people and tell lies deliberately in order to deceive others. These deceivers can be both intelligent and clever; consequently, one can argue that the other writings of such people too were intentionally meant to deceive others. Following this rationale, we must have a more precise look at the writings in this book.

If the readers of these lines have another alternative reading of the facts that I have mentioned, I would gratefully listen to them and extend my apologies in case they could challenge my views. Otherwise it would mean that they have admitted that my views are correct.

Even though the Christian clergies who had recognized these Gospels had realized this contradiction, they preferred to remain silent to protect their own interests and positions, because they were earning their livelihood out of it. I have talked to many Christian clergies in person, and they honestly and sincerely confess that they had never thought about this point, and I never doubted their honesty. It seems that these people suffer from a kind of blindness because after a while of staying in a place, one is no longer capable of seeing the problems and shortcomings of that place. Particularly, when people believe in something as sacred as a religion, they become completely blind and just start seeing its good sides, looking for its positive aspects, and nothing else. Such people cannot have an independent look at that belief or that book with an open mind.

This introduction to the New Testament raises the possibility that it was Jews who wrote the New Testament and included a part of their own stories in the Mandaeans' story. In other words, the New Testament might be the amalgamation of Judaism and Mandaean faith (and possibly some other faiths common in that region) written by those Jews who were fed up with the endless viciousness of the Judaism introduced in the Old Testament and wanted to benefit from the peaceful nature and peaceful life style of Mandaean people.

On the other hand, if it is argued that Jesus Christ's father is God, then it is ridiculous to say that Jesus was a Jew from his father's side, because that is to claim that the Glorious God that we are all talking about -who has created this magnificent world- was himself a Jew!

If Jesus Christ is God's son, why should we call him a Jew unless we claim that God was a Jew too!? And if both God and Jesus Christ were Jews, what was the necessity to introduce another religion? Based on this rationale, the necessity of creating another religion disappears and everyone must convert to Judaism as God and his son were Jews, until and unless we assume another hypothesis that:

God (Jesus Christ) and his mother were Mandaean and in comparison to Joseph (Mary's husband, who was a Jew) they were less valued. But the main hypothesis which is based on the information existing in this book is that: Those Jews who made up a new religion by using Mandaean ideas, stories and myths, tried to place their own previous religion within this new religion.

<u>But why is there no mention of Mandaeans?</u>

The reason is the brutal massacre of Mandaeans by Jews, who accordingly expatriated them to Iraq and southern areas of Iran (Khuzestan) near Euphrates and Tigris Rivers. Today Mandaeans reside in these areas. Therefore, if they would have mentioned anything about Mandaeans, they had to admit the fact that Jesus Christ was not a Jew but Mandaean. Following such a confession, they also had to expose other facts, which would have put their background under a question mark. The following lines will develop these points further:

In the New Testament, the origins of Mary are not obvious. That is to say, there is no generation tree of Mary to prove her Jewish origins. Neither there, or in other sources, can we see any hint about the family relationships between Mary and Joseph from which we can indirectly recognize her as a Jew. Mary's life in the New Testament is vague. Therefore, we must explore the other possibilities. In order to do this, some basic points should be examined one by one.

Saint Matthew's Gospel:

Chapter 1:

Verse 18: "Now the birth of Jesus Christ was on this wise: When as his mother Mary was espoused to Joseph, before they came together, she was found with child of the Holy Ghost"

Verse 19: "Then Joseph her husband, being just a man, and not willing to make her a public example, was minded to put her away privily".

Verse 20: "But while he thought on these things, behold, the angel of the Lord appeared unto him in a dream, saying, Joseph, thou son of David, fear not to take unto thee Mary thy wife: for that which is conceived in her is of the Holy Ghost".

Verse 21: "And she shall bring forth a son, and thou shalt call his name JESUS: for he shall save his people from their sins".

Verse 22: "Now all this was done, that it might be fulfilled which was spoken of the Lord by the prophet, saying,

Verse 23: "Behold, a virgin shall be with child and shall bring forth a son and they shall call his name Em-man'u-el, which being interpreted is, God with us."

Verse 24: "Then Joseph being raised from sleep did as the angel of the Lord had bidden him, and took unto him his wife:

Verse 25: "And knew her not till she had brought forth

her firstborn son: and he called his name JESUS.

Note: Unlike Greek people, Jews did not believe in marriage with God, and God's child etc., so they could not at all accept that Mary had married to God and consequently had given birth to God's child. As a result, and according to Jewish teachings, she should have been stoned, but she was not. The only explanation to justify this contradiction is to accept that Mary and her husband Joseph were not Jews.

<u>Explanation:</u>

In the Arabic text of the New Testament, rather than "Jesus" the term يسـوع (Jesu or in Arabic yesaa) has been adopted. Based on this ground, they are called يسـوعيون or يسـوعيان (Jesuits in Arabic yesaaien). The word Yesaa is connected to Messiah or in other language Meshia having relation with touching or washing body with water or liquid. In Arabic one word can conjugate in ten times as well as this word.

"Jesu" means "pure" which is the same as "Ješu" in Hebrew. This supports the idea that "Jesus" or "Jesu" is not a fully Hebrew name and must have been borrowed from a language related to Hebrew. However, it was not "Jašu" which went to the West rather, "Jasu" from which they derived the name "Jesus". Coincidently, "Jesus" is pronounced in its correct form in Swedish where the letter /J/ represents the sound /y/ not /d**j** /.

In addition, in case we replace the sound /š/ with /s/, we will come up with the name "Ješu" which does not exist in Arabic language at all. The name "Jesus" has turned to "Jose" in Spanish where the letter /J/ represents the sound /x/. The reason for this is that when the Spanish people saw this name in Latin alphabet, they pronounced it according to their own language.

Another contradictory point to mention is that in verse 18, Mary and Joseph are introduced as fiancées, but in verse 19, namely the next verse (only 15 words ahead) they are introduced as husband and wife. We know that being husband and wife bear sexual relations. In this case, if we accept Mary and Joseph as couple (according to verse 19), we have automatically rejected Mary's being a virgin.

-Another point that to be dealt with in the following lines is the name "Imanuel- Emanuel" which will be compared with some other key words.

Up to now, we came up with this argument that the absence of Mary's generation tree evokes great doubt. However, in Matthew's Gospel, there is a mention of one of the relatives of Mary called Elisabeth (originally in Arabic or in Hebrew Al yasa-bat but in West, this name has became Elizabeth and as soon as it came back to this region again, it was accepted and used in its new form as Elizabeth) who was Zachariya's wife and their son was "John" the Baptist. John became an eminent Baptist so that Jesus Christ looked for him enthusiastically. But why? Among Jews baptism was not common; therefore, why should have Jesus been looking for baptism?! According to the New Testament, when they decided to name the child "John", her kindred protested and said what a strange name it was and argued that such a name did not exist among them. This point illustrates that John's family, who were Mary's relatives, were not Jews, and that is why they had selected a name which was unfamiliar for the Jewish authors of the New Testament, who represented this as a protest of the people of that time to this name.

The relationship between John/Yahya and Jesus

Saint Luke's Gospel talks about John's birth, naming, and food. Throughout Elisabeth's pregnancy, until John was born, Zachariya (John's father) with the order of the angel became dumb and compliant. Elisabeth hid her pregnancy up to the fifth month. In the sixth month of her pregnancy, the angel came in unto Mary (the Virgin), Joseph's fiancé, and announced that she would be pregnant and deliver a son who should be named "Jesus".

Saint Luke's Gospel

Chapter 1:

Verse 31: "And, behold, thou shalt conceive in thy womb, and bring forth a son, and shalt call his name JESUS".

Here, it must be noted that:

According to Luke's Gospel, Jesus Christ's name was revealed to Mary prior to his birth while according to verse 21 of Saint Matthew's Gospel (which was quoted earlier) Jesus Christ's name was revealed to Joseph - Mary's husband- in his dreams. This adds another contradiction to those discussed earlier. However, there is one more contradictory point.

Saint Luke's Gospel

Chapter 1:

Verse 32: "he shall be great, and shall be called the Son of the Highest: and the Lord God shall give unto him the throne of his father David"

It is important to focus on this contradiction because Jesus was not related to David, and why therefore should it have read "throne of his father David". These are all the points which mislead the people into believing in the Jewish origin of Jesus and his mother Mary.

Verse 33: "And he shall reign over the house of Jacob for ever; and of his kingdom there shall be no end."

Verse 34: "then said Mary unto the angel, how shall this be, seeing I know not a man?

Verse 35: " And the angel answered and said unto her, The Holy Ghost shall come upon thee, and the power of the Highest shall overshadow thee: therefore also that holy thing which shall be born of thee shall be called the Son of God."

Verse 36: "And, behold, thy cousin Elizabeth, she hath also conceived a son in her old age: and this is the sixth month with her, who was called barren".

In this verse, it is explicitly written "thy cousin Elisabeth", therefore it can be inferred that Mary and Elizabeth were relatives, and consequently they believed in the same religion. It would become easier to realize whether Mary was a Jew or Mandaean. In case

Elisabeth and her husband Zacharia were Jews, their generation tree would definitely have been mentioned.

Nevertheless, if Jesus Christ was meant to rule over Jacob's successors, (verse 33) then there was and there is no necessity for the continuation of Judaism, and those who remained Jew were, and still are, Jesus Christ's enemy.

Mary went to salute Elizabeth and as soon as the baby (John) heard Mary's voice, he began to leap.

Verse 56: "And Mary abode with her about three months, and returned to her own house".

Elizabeth delivered a son who was supposed to be circumcised on the eighth day.

Verse 59: "And it came to pass, that on the eighth day they came to circumcise the child; and they called him Zacharias, after the name of his father."

Verse 60: "And his mother answered and said, Not so; but he shall be called john".

Verse 61: "And they said unto her, There is none of thy kindred that is called by this name".

Verse 62: "And they made signs to his father, how he would have him called".

Verse 63: "And he asked for a writing table and wrote, saying, His name is John. And they marveled all".

Here, the issue of name is indicative of the ethnic and religious associations that authors were not able to hide. They were not able to choose a name other than John, which was not Jewish. The name Yahya is derived from Hay هیی / حیی "Hayyi", the Mandaean great God.

On the other hand, if Yahya was a Jew and circumcised, why should he has been Baptist? Jews do not follow the ritual of baptizing, so therefore circumcising John is a fake story made up to portray him as a Jew.

Note: In Arabic and English versions of The New Testament, Yahya is quoted as Johanna. In Persian is "Yahya" and in Mandaean scriptures, his complete name is "Yahya Johanna".

The second chapter deals with Jesus Christ's birth. Caesar Augustus released a decree that everyone should be registered (for paying taxes). Consequently, Joseph left Galilee to Bethlehem where Mary was located.

Saint Luke's Gospel

Chapter 2

Verse 5: "To be taxed with Mary his espoused wife, being great with child."

…

Verse 21: "And when eight days were accomplished for the circumcising of the child, his name was called JESUS, which was so named of the angel before he was conceived in the womb."

Verse 22: "And when the days of her purification according to the Law of Moses were accomplished, they brought him to Jerusalem to present him to the Lord:"

Verse 23: (As it is written in the law of the Lord, Every

male that openeth the womb shall be called holy to God ;)

Verse 24: "And to offer a sacrifice according to that which is said in the law of the Lord, A pair of turtledoves, or two young pigeons."

Sacrificing a bird is a Mandaean ritual!

Mandaean believers don't usually eat the animals which walk on earth, except a ram lamb; consequently, their food is mainly comprised of birds and seafoods. As a result, the animal they used to choose for sacrificing should have been one of these two types, and since it was not possible to spill the blood of a fish as a sacrifice, they used to choose their sacrifice from among birds.

For Mandaeans, a sacrifice was either a pigeon or a turtledove. They did not even sacrifice poultry, because they were not capable of flying, although they looked like birds. In contrast, pigeon and turtledove could fly to the sky and this associated them with a sense of spirituality, which made them suitable for being selected for sacrifice. That is why sacrificing turtledoves and pigeons are stated in the Gospel overtly.

Saint Luke's Gospel

Chapter 2

Verse 24: "And to offer a sacrifice according to that which is said in the law of the Lord, A pair of turtledoves, or two young pigeons."

This is also another significant point, which sheds light on the Mandaean origins of Jesus Christ. In case Jesus Christ and his mother were Jews (of course God or God's son cannot have a religion), they should have offered their sacrifice according to the Jewish rituals. This is an evidence which indicates that they were Mandaeans not Jews. Of course if there really existed a Jesus Christ and following that the circumcision story, on the eighth day of his birth, Jesus was not capable of making a decision regardless of what religion he had. And in fact, circumcising Jesus was not done according to Mary's own wishes.

In addition, in verses 23 and 24 there is a mention of Lords' Law not Moses' Law. In Arabic gospel it is stated:

" وليقدما ذبيحه كما يوصى فى شريعه رب ((زوجى يمام، او فرخى حمام)). "

whose translation in Persian is exactly "Lord's Law."

The question is this: Is Moses' Law equal to Lord's law? And if it is, which God? If there is a difference between Moses' Law and Lord's Law, then what would the reading and interpretation of this story be? For Christians, Moses' Law should not have been equal to God's law, otherwise it was not necessary for Jesus Christ to bring a new law. Jesus Christ was taken to Jerusalem according to Moses' Law but they offered their sacrifice according to God's Law, which was in accordance with Mandaean Law, not Moses' Law.

<u>Conclusion: Lord's Law is Mandaean</u>

If Jesus Christ's mother, i.e. Mary, was a Jew, the sacrifice should have been performed according to Jewish traditions, and since this was not the case, it means that they were not Jews but Mandaeans.

I should point out that at that time, Mandaeans were settled in Jerusalem.

Chapter 29 of the Old Testament, Exodus, has extensively explained the sacrificing rituals and the animals selected for this purpose i.e. rams and cattle. There, when Yahweh gave these orders to Moses, there was no mention of birds as sacrifices.

<u>Divorce does not exist among Mandaeans!</u>

A new look at the New Testament

<u>Saint Mathew's Gospel</u>

Chapter 5

32: But I say unto you, That whosoever shall put away his wife, saving for the cause of fornication, causeth her to commit adultery: and whosoever shall marry her that is divorced committeth adultery.

Among Mandaean people, getting divorce is prohibited and they still try to maintain this tradition despite all the changes happening in the world and in human societies, while among Jews, divorce was a common tradition. Therefore, Jesus Christ made such a statement due to his being Mandaean. It was due to Jesus Christ's ban on divorce in this verse that getting divorce is now prohibited among Catholics.

<u>Yahya's clothing and food</u>

<u>Mathew's Gospel</u>

Chapter 3

Verse 4: And the same John had his raiment of camel's hair, and a leathern girdle about his loins; and his meal was locusts and wild honey.

The point made about Yahya's food reveals some truths about his religion and ethnicity. Those who are not familiar with the issue might have their own reading and interpretation but the fact of the matter is something different.

As mentioned before, Yahya (John) was Mandaean and Mandaeans did not feed on the animals which walked on the earth as considered dirty (Nejes) نجس except rarely rams. So as a Mandaean, he used to eat locusts, which were considered flying creatures. If Yahya was a Jew (Arab), he could have eaten the animals which walked on the earth. The food type can be considered as an indicator of cultural, ethnic, national, and religious characteristics. Yahya's cloth, which was made of camel hair, was very similar to "suf"; a cloth put on by Sufis (mystics). According to some scholars, the name "Sufi" itself is derived from the name of this cloth.

<u>Investigating Yahya's name</u>

The name "Yahya" is another issue that is open to debate. According to the Persian book "Tamidiyane Gharib", written by Mehrdad Arabestani, and published jointly by the Organization of Cultural Heritage and Nashre Afkar (Afkar Publisher) In Iran, the term "هیی" "Hayyi" means "life", which is the name of Mandaean God. Aramaic script used by Mandaeans does not have the letter "ح", rather the letter "ه". In this case both "حیی" and "هیی" must be considered as the same. Consequently, we can write "یحیی" either as "یحیی" or " یه هیی" . Both "حیی" and "هیی" are the same. In <u>Mandaean scriptures, Yahya's name has been cited as Yahya Johanna</u>. In western sources, Yahya has been eliminated and only Johanna is used. This name in different places is pronounced in different ways. For instance, since in Swedish the sound /j/ is pronounced as /y/, the Swedish version of name Yahya namely, Johan is therefore pronounced similarly to Yahya as cited in Mandaean scriptures.

Swedish: Johannes

English: John

German: Johannes

French: Jean

Arabic: Johanna   یوحنا

Persian: Yahya   یحیی

Same as "Jesus" which in Swedish pronounce is "yesus"

Jesus Christ's baptism by Yahya and its comparison to circumcision: Circumcision did not exist, and still does not exist, among Mandaeans!

Saint Mathew's Gospel

Chapter 3

Verse 13: Then cometh Jesus from Galilee to Jordan unto John, to be baptized of him.

14: But John forbad him, saying, I have need to be baptized of thee, and comest thou to me?

15: And Jesus answering said unto him, suffer *it to be so* now: for thus it becometh us to fulfill all righteousness. Then he suffered him.

16: And Jesus, when he was baptized, went up straightway out of the water: and, lo, the heavens were opened unto him, and he saw the Spirit of God descending like a dove, and lightening upon him."

Based on these verses, Jesus was baptized by a Mandaean and through this event; the heaven was opened unto him. It should therefore be pointed out that it was following Jesus Christ's baptism that heaven was opened unto him, not his circumcision. This is indicative of the superiority of baptism as a Mandaean ritual over circumcision, which was a Jewish tradition.

Another point to mention is that he observed God's Spirit as a dove. This adds to the significance of dove and its being elected as a sacrifice. Since there is no bond between two traditions of circumcision and baptism as features of the two different religions, therefore, while writing the Bible, only one of these two accounts must be considered as true and the other one as false. In addition since it was explicitly cited that the heaven was opened after baptism, and therefore the account of circumcision is unreal and was probably included in the Bible later on.

Being baptized was not an obligatory ritual among Jews but it was a mandatory tradition among Mandaean people. Jews and Arabs, whose ancestors were the same as the ancestors of Mohammed the Prophet, did not have the tradition of baptism, which is why this tradition is not a part of Islam. On the contrary; among Muslims and Jews, the requirement for converting to Islam or Judaism, even at a mature age, is to be circumcised, while under both Christian and Mandaean faiths the requirement for converting to Christianity or Mandaeism faith is baptism.

It must be noted that at present, Judaism is a faith not a race or an ethnicity. The requirement to join to a nation or a group of people is not to have circumcision or baptism. These traditions are peculiar to religious conversions. Being a member of a community or nation is a process which takes place through blood relationships like getting married into them, living among them for a long time and accepting their culture and other features. In some cases, one can never be a real member of that community after just ten years of living with them; in addition, some of these ethnicities may not even believe in certain religions or rituals.

On the other hand, Jesus Christ could not have looked for Mandaean Yahya all over that region to get baptised, because his father was the Lord. In addition, if his mother was a Jew, she would not have talked to him about baptism and he would not have had any idea about it. As it is the case, even in the present time, that when one is born into a family with a certain religion, one has hardly any information about other religions and it is exactly due to this reason that for almost two millennia, no one has been curious to conduct an in-depth research like this one about Jesus Christ's origins. The reason is that there is no mention of other religions in families and even if there is, it is a biased one, which mainly condemns other religions. Moreover, they may not often see the books of other religions, let alone read them. They may even destroy them if they have the chance to do so. We should not forget the book burners!

It might be necessary to point out here that the reason I came up with these findings was partly due to the way my family, in particular my father, was. My father was not a religiously biased person, and since my childhood, there used to be both the Old Testament and New Testament in our house, and I had the chance to read them both along with Quran.

In any case, even if we have to accept Jesus Christ's circumcision story, it can be justified in this way that his circumcision was carried out upon the will or recommendation of Joseph his mothers husband, who was probably – though not definitely- a Jew.

My own point of view is that they have made up these stories and have done their best to make it look real; however, all the contradictions observed in them are obvious. Jesus Christ did not accept circumcision when he became mature.

The Parting of the sea by Moses and walking on water by Jesus:

 How could the parting of the sea (river) by Moses happen? Even if we would partially accept the story that these people crossed the river through Moses' miracle, it still needs to be justified in some ways. By that time, they were still not known as Jews. Their being called Jewish people happens centuries later when they migrated from Egypt and settled in Palestine. This time also coincides with the disappearance of ten of the twelve tribes.

Jews who were Arab (nomads) did not have much contact with water in their environment and had almost no knowledge about swimming and passing through the water. Therefore, it is probable that Moses did it (Moses was an Egyptian not Arab and even his name meant "taken from water" in Egyptian. Even the tradition of circumcision was passed to Jews from Egyptians through Moses) and his people crossed the river by making a bridge, boat or blowing sheepskin. However, the exaggerated and embellished memory of these people (of course the myth of all nations has been formed and developed in this manner) has likened this action to parting the river. Since the Suez Canal was not built by that time, consequently, Moses and the Israelites (Bani Israel) entered Sinai Peninsula through land, and they probably passed some small rivers in that area. It must be pointed out that according to the Old Testament; the land promised to Jews extends between waters. The land promised to Jews extends from the Mediterranean and the Red Sea up to the Euphrates River (west of Tigris River) in Iraq.

In order to understand this feature of Judaism, we must compare it with stories of some centuries later and the advent of Islam. The story of the Old Testament belongs to many years before that but by the advent of Islam; the world had gone through remarkable changes and had achieved many significant advances. However, when Islam's army set off to conquer Iran, Omar, the Caliphate of that time wrote a letter to his commander according to Arab traditions and advised him against crossing the Euphrates and Tigris, but by the time the letter arrived, the army had already crossed the river.

Comparing the story about Jesus and Moses clarifies the result. Contrary to Arabs, who were not familiar with water, Mandaeans used to settle near streams and therefore they knew how to swim. For this reason, when Jews saw Jesus Christ swimming in water without drowning, they said that he could float and walk on water. Here, playing with the words seems simple and understandable - however, when the story keeps on being narrated in such a way for centuries, then people gradually forget about the "swimming" and make hundreds of interpretations like "walking on water". Comparing Moses' life with Jesus Christ's life is in fact comparing the nomad Arabs and lowland Mandaeans. Looking at the issue from this point of view can also lead to the conclusion that Jesus Christ could not have been a nomad Arab, but rather a lowland Mandaean.

Jews killed Jesus Christ:

According to the New Testament and the historical evidence and reasons, killing the Mandaean Jesus Christ and other Mandaeans was carried out by Jews not Romans. Neither were Jews capable of admitting the murder of Jesus Christ nor the Mandaeans rejecting it. That is why the New Testament discusses this issue in an ambiguous way. That Jews murdered Jesus Christ could be better inferred from Mandaean books. Unfortunately, as Mandaeans did not like their holy book to be available for others, (similar to Zoroastrians whose holy book just became available for all during the past two centuries) and refrained from showing their book to others, it was consequently impossible to have access to this information and the real inferences contained in those writings.

One of the holy books of Mandaeans is "Mandaean book of John" or Adrāšā Ad Yahya. An excerpt from this book, which has been mentioned in a book called "Sabeine Rastin" (The real Mandaean- Sabeine is another name for the Mandaean people but has deferent meaning), by: Adel Shirali, 1389 Iran, p. 93, is quoted below:

"Koheins dreamt that a star shined in the sky of Jerusalem and settled beside Nishbai, John's mother. The flames of the fire began glowing near Zachariya's house, and three flames began glowing before the Jews' temple in Jerusalem. The holy temple of Israelites was filled with dust and smoke, a lot of noise arose, the fruits of the trees began to move about and an arrow of fire appeared in the sky of Jerusalem." (Mandaean book of John, P.47).

Jewish koheins (Coheins) looked for the interpretation of this dream and from among four great dream interpreters, "Jolekh" was selected. A messenger was sent to him and he wrote them a letter in return.

"Be alarmed **if** Nishbai's child is born in Jerusalem and **what a** poor Torah if John is born in Jerusalem."

Note: Nishbai is the name of John's mother.

The top kohein (Cohein) of Jews who was called Alaazar asked Zachariya to leave Jerusalem but Zachariya did not know why. Zachariya and his family lived in Jerusalem. (In order to realize that Jerusalem was not only the settlement for Jews, and rather many Mandaeans too, see the story of Jesus Christ's going to Jerusalem for sacrificing). Finally, John was born and the kohein's dream came true. They went to Zachariya's house and decided to name the baby "Yakef", or "Zatan" but Nishbai protested and said she did not ask them to select a name for her child. Koheins got irritated and left their house with hearts full of hatred. The birthday of John is one of the Mandaean religious holidays known as "Dehwa de Mana". Every year on this occasion, Mandaeans hold festivals and baptize their children. (Mandaean book no.46, p.2)

Next day, koheins attacked Zachariya's house to kill John but they could not find him. The events of John's life until his twenty-two years of age is another period. In "Haran Gawaita" which is another Mandaean source, this period has been mentioned. In this source, it has been quoted that in order to save John's life, an angel known as Uthra Anoš was tasked to protect John. Anoš took John to a mountain known as "Parvan Tavar Havara" or White Mountain. The place and the identity of the mountain is not known. According to Mandaean beliefs, John was hidden until he was twenty two years old. During this period, he used to drink holy water (flowing water) and fed from the extract of a tree, which fed John like a nanny. When he was seven years old, uthra Anoš taught him Mandaean alphabet known as "a-be-ge-de" (ا-ب-گ-د) which seems to be equivalent to the "Abjad" alphabet. While he was hidden, he learnt the teachings of the Mandaean faith. (Book of John, p.91)

Note: I could not find the meaning and the etymology of the names "Yakef" and "zatan" but here, by holy water it is meant the "flowing water". In such a case, the well water or lake water could not be holy. Arabs (nomads) used to drink from wells and lake water. John did not baptize even in Galilee lake because its water was not running, and as a result, it was not considered as holy. He used to baptize in the River Jordan.

This 22 years disappearance of John can compare with the Jesus disappearance.

Mandaeans believe that John was hidden until 22 years of age in order to protect himself from the people of Moses. Then by God's will his period of being hidden came to an end and he appeared in Jerusalem. On a Sunday in Jerusalem, a voice was heard that said a great man was about to come. "A messenger has come to Jerusalem whose nose and mouth seems like Nishbai, and his body features are like her husband Zacharya. Nishbai left the house in worry and anxiety running towards the owner of the voice. When she looked at the 22 year-old young man, she realized that he was her own lost and hidden child, John. She hugged him, her waiting came to an end and finally found her child." (Ginza Raba, p, 190-191).

Note: paying attention to Sunday and its significance!

The story of being hidden has influenced Muslims too and they have made up such stories for their holy people. After his reappearance in Jerusalem, John lived all his time beside Mandaean people and spent all his life to teach them Mandaean religious teachings. In fact, a new era of his life began with his reappearance after being hidden. John was not interested in getting married, however the Mandaean deities realized that their population would decrease in this way. Nevertheless, John always promoted marriage in his preachings, though in his own case, he used to say that "if I get married, it might stop me from praying to God, and I might be in dreams when the night comes".

Here, we can relate that to avoiding marriage among some Christians (man or woman) which does not originate from Judaism as they did not believe in it, instead it was a tradition which was rooted in Mandaean faith. Deities insisted on his getting married but he resisted until a voice from heaven was revealed unto him:

"Thou, John, get married and let your longing come to tranquility. Pray your God on Sundays and Thursdays and avoid anything which is in the void world". Hearing the revelation, which was from God, John got married and had many children. John's death happened near the shore while he was baptizing.

"Manda d-Hayyi" the great angel, was assigned to take his soul. He descended to him as a three year-old child and asked for baptism. After some discussion, John admitted him but as Manda d-Hayyi was taking a step towards Jordan River, the river was stepping backward. (Ginza Rba, p. 192- 5)

John realized that it was a death angel and he took the angel's hand with all his heart to set his soul free. The interesting point to mention is that when someone cannot touch the streaming water, it means the time for his/her death has arrived. By seeing his own corpse, John felt sad. Seeing his sorrow, Manda d-Hayyi told him: "why did you become sad for this blood and flesh? I can send you back to this flesh cover if you want". John answered: "I am sad because I am going to leave my children and can't teach them any further".

Manda d-Hayyi said: "I know what is going on in your heart and why you are sad"

John's soul passed the world of light along with Manda d-Hayyi and passed through the stages with the angels. He could reach to such a high point with the power of his faith. (Book of John, p, 67, 77-7)

Another point here is to reach to God by virtue. This is the Gnosis or Manda whose aim is to reach to God, and John succeeded in achieving this aim. To reach to God also exists in Islamic Gnosis. However, some Shiites (people following Ali) consider it blasphemy, and that is why they killed Hallaj.

The conclusion we can draw from this story is that John was prosecuted and was under pressure of death by Jews - so how could it be possible that someone of Jewish origin looked for such a person to receive baptism from? Therefore, Jesus Christ was not originally Jewish; rather he also was from the same people John belonged to – namely, Mandaeans.

<u>Jesus Christ' story was a Mandaean story</u>

John's teachings on theology and ethics exists among Mandaean people. However, the most important conclusion that we can draw, is that Jewish people not (Romans) took their revenge from Jesus Christ and murdered him. There are some discussions on the way Jesus Christ was crucified. For instance, the way he was crucified was not in Roman style because they had nailed his hands, which is against roman style. Romans used to fix the hands on the cross with a strap. There are some other issues which have been investigated by others previously and I see no need to repeat those researches here.

Jews were not satisfied only with killing Jesus Christ, they also made vast massacres among the Mandaean people, and forced them to expatriate from their lands in order to protect their lives. They migrated to the south of Iran and Iraq and settled near the Euphrates, Tigris and Karon rivers.

In comparison to other stories, Johanna's Gospel and John's revelations make more mentions of Jesus Christ's being threatened to death. Other Gospels also make direct mention of Jesus Christ's being killed by Jews. Jews embarked on stoning Jesus Christ many times, for instance:

John's Gospel

Chapter 8:

This chapter deals with Jesus Christ's discussion with Jews about their ancestors. From verse 40 onward, their discussion becomes harsher. Jews told Jesus Christ that they were not adulterate (verse 41). It seems that in this verse, ironically, Jews' intention was to say that it was Jesus Christ who was an adulterate not Jews.

Jews argued that their father was God but Jesus Christ argued that their father was the devil. Jews argued that Jesus Christ had a devil inside him and wanted to stone him.

Verse 59: then took they up stones to cast at him: but Jesus hid himself, and went out of the temple, going through the midst of them, and so passed by.

John's Gospel

Chapter 10

Verse 30: I and my father are one.

Verse 31: then the Jews took up stones again to stone him.

Verse 32: Jesus answered them, many good works have I shewded you from my father; for which of those works do ye stone me?

Verse 33: the Jews answered him, saying, For a good work we stone thee not; but for blasphemy; and because that thou, being a man makest thyself God.

Verse 39: therefor they sought again to take him: but he escaped out of their hand,

There are many instances in the New Testament where it is mentioned that Jews wanted to hurt or stone Jesus Christ. It can be inferred from these threats that Jesus Christ was not Jewish because: Jews used to call anyone preaching a few words a "messenger". They even call the people like Marx, Lenin and Spinoza "messengers" and don't threaten them. As a result, Jesus Christ must have been non-Jewish as he was threatened with death and finally murdered.

Some points about John's Gospel

1-There are no direct religious instructions, rituals or social regulations in John's Gospel.

2-Mostly it is an account about Jesus Christ's self grandiosity as it is always the case with other heads of the faiths specially Sufis.

3-The issue of being father and son is mentioned more in this Gospel in comparison to other Gospels.

4-Jews' violence towards Jesus Christ is indicated more in this Gospel so that they embark on killing him many times and Jesus Christ becomes forced to migrate to Galilee.

5-It is only in this Gospel where there is a mention of Greeks.

6-Some of the Greek and Roman names, which are mentioned as Jewish, illustrate that these people had accepted Judaism, as a result the same people created the new religion known as Christianity.

Matthew: Eli, Eli, lema sabachthani

Mark: Eloi, Eloi, lama sabachthani

In Persian:

انجيل متى: "ايلى ايلى، لما سبقتنى"

انجيل مرقس: "ايلوئى، ايلوئى لما سبقتنى"

In Arabic:

الانجيل كما دونه متى: "ايلى ايلى، لما شبقتنى"

الانجيل كما دونه مرقس: "الوى الوى، لما شبقتنى"

These are the only words which are directly mentioned by Jesus Christ. These words are not Hebrew (Jewish language) but Aramaic.

The last and the most robust evidence, which rejects the Jewish origin of Jesus Christ, are words which are directly quoted by him. These words reveal his language, however the confusions regarding these words are significant and it seems that they are not Hebrew. In order to understand the difference between ايـل (il) and ئيـل (el), one should have knowledge about some other issues as well. In an article which I have written earlier, I have explained how the term ﻧﯿـﻞ (el) which refers to the God of Babylonian people spread among other people including Jewish people and then through time it turned to "ال" (al), (alle) "الـﻪ" and "الله" (Allah). Here the same term is used as "اﯾـﻞ" (el) and "اﯾﻠـﻮ" (elu) where each of which is an accent of Arabic or Aramaic language.

If these words had been intelligible for the Jewish people of the time when the book was written, there would not have been a need for writing its exact translation.

Bab/ باب is a word which means "gate" and is still used in Arabic language.

El/ ﻧﯿﻞ means God and "bab-el " meant "God's gate" or "the gate to reach to God". Following the same rationale, still there are many people who consider themselves as "the gate to reach to God" so that in order to get to God, one should pass through them.

It should be taken into consideration that the Hebrew accent or language is closer to Arabs and they can learn each others' accents quickly. The significance of this sentence is so great that no matter into which language the New Testament has been translated, this phrase has been quoted exactly the same way. When Jesus Christ was crucified, he uttered these words: اﯾﻠﻰ اﯾﻠﻰ /Eli Eli/.

<u>Mathew's Gospel</u>

Chapter 27

Verse 46 in Arabic:

ونحو الساعه الثالثه صرخ يسوع اى " الهى، الهى، لماذا تركتنى؟ "
بصوت عظيم "ايلى، ايلى، لما شبقتنى؟ "

Verse 46 in Swedish:

Vid nionde timmen ropade Jesus med hög röst: "Eli, Eli, lema sabachtani?" (vilket betyder: Min Gud, min Gud, varför har du över givit mig?).

Verse 46 according to King James translation of Bible:

And about the ninth hour Jesus cried with loud Voice, saying, E´li, E´li, la´ma sa-bach´tha-ni? That is to say, My God, My God, why hast thou forsaken me?

Verse 46 in German:

Und um die neunte stunde schrie Jesus laut: Eli, Eli, lama asabtani? Das heißt: Mein Gott, mein gott, warum hast du mich verlassen?

Verse 46 in French:

Et, vers la neuvième heure, Jésus s'écria d'une voix forte: Eli, Eli, lama sabachtani? c'est-à-dire: Mon Dieu, mon Dieu, pourquoi m'as-tu abandonné?

Elo Elo :ايلــو ايلــو

Saint Mark's Gospel

Chapter 15

Verse 34: And at the ninth hour Jesus cries with a loud voice, saying, E-lo'i, E-lo'i, la'ma sa-bah'tha-ni? which is, being interpreted, My God, My God, why hast thou forsaken me?

Verse 34 in Arabic:

و فى الساعه الثالثه، صرخ يسوع بصوت عظيم: " الوى الوى، لما شبقتنى؟" اى "الهى الهى، لماذا تركتنى؟"

Verse 34 in English:

And at the ninth hour Jesus cried with a loud voice, saying, Eloi, Eloi, lama sabachthani? Which is, why hast thou forsaken me?

Verse 34 in Swedish:

Och vid nionde timmen ropade Jesus med hög röst: "Eloi, Eloi, lema sabachtani?" (Det betyder: Min Gud, min gud varför har du övergivit mig?).

Verse 34 in German:

Und zu der neunten stunde rief Jesus laut: Eli, Eli, lama asabtani? Das heiβt übersetzt: Mein Gott, mein Gott, warum hast du mich verssen?

Verse 34 in French:

 Et á la neuvième heure, Jésus s'écria d'une voix forte: Eloï, Eloï, lama sabachtani? ce qui signifie: Mon Dieu, mon Dieu, pourguoi m'as-tu abandonné?

ئيل /El/

In order to clarify the difference between El and Elo some instances of both terms must be mentioned.

Mathew's Gospel

Chapter 1

Verse 23: Behold, a virgin shall be with child and shall bring forth a son, and they shall call his name Em-man´u-el, which being interpreted is, God with us.

Here El means God.

Arabic: عمانوئيل

English: Emma nu el

Swedish: Imma nu el

French: d´emma nu el

Saint Luke's Gospel

Chapter 1

Verse 19: And the angel answering said unto him, I am Gabriel, that stand in the presence of God; and am sent to speak unto thee, and to shew thee these glad tidings.

Arabic

فاجابه الملک: " انا جبرائیل، الواقف...

King James' English translation of Bible:

And the angel answering said unto him, I am Gabri el, that …"

Swedish:

Ängeln svarade honom: "Jag är Gabri el…".

German:

Der Engel antwortete und sprach steht zu ihm: Ich bin Gabri el, …

When Jesus calls God (not his father), he utters the words "Der Engel antwortete und sprach steht zu ihm: Ich bin Gabri el, …" El, or "ايلــو" Elo in his own language but since it is quoted in Jews ordinary language it is "ئيـــل".

Nevertheless, the accent and language difference is obvious and reveals that Jesus Christ's' language and accent was different from Hebrew speaking Jews, so that Jewish writers of the Bible could not deny it and had no other way than translating them. Even the two terms, شبقتنى و سبقتنى / sabaghtani/,/shabaghtani/ are also indicative of such differences.

Some basic but significant points:

> 1- One significant point worth mentioning is that if Jesus Christ had been God's son, why didn't he address himself or his father rather than directly addressing God when he was crying out in pain? This direct quotation from Jesus Christ does not indicate in any way that there was a father-son or other family relationships between him and God, rather it is the imploring of a believer in God like any other believer.

2- Another point to mention is that in Mark's Gospel and Matthew's Gospel, God's name is written in two ways.

3- In order to investigate and understand the terms "ايلى" /Eli/ or "ايلوى" /Eloi/ and to write and pronounce them correctly, we should take the Arabic version of the Bible as the basis for this investigation because it was their language and script. In addition, the purpose of putting forward this issue is to show that the quotations by Jesus Christ were not in Hebrew language rather in other language Aramaic even in two dialects.

For instance, as it is seen, the name of two countries "Iran" and "Iraq" are too similar when they are written in the Latin alphabet but very different when written in Arabic alphabet (عراق-ايران). When uttering the name of these countries, it is too hard to distinguish between them until and unless one puts stress on the last sound or associates the name of the country with the name of the person who comes from there.

4- In all Gospels, which have been written in different languages, the time when Jesus Christ starts crying out is 9 o'clock, but in Arabic translation it is 3 o'clock. This difference is explained in Saint Luke's Gospel as follows:

Saint Luke's Gospel

Chapter 23

Verse 44: And it was about the sixth hour, and there was a darkness over all the earth until the ninth hour.

Verse 45: And the sun was darkened, and the veil of the temple was rent in the midst.

Arabic version:

Verse 44:

و نحو الساعه السادسه (الثانيه عشره ظهرا)، حل الظلام على الارض كلها حتى الساعه التاسعه (الثالثه بعد الظهر)

Verse 45:

واظلمت الشمس، وانشطر ستار الهيكل من الوسط.

Here the explanation clarifies what it is meant by 3 o'clock in Saint Mark and Saint Mathew's Gospel and how it is the same as 9 o'clock in other languages.

However, a different point among Gospels is observed here:

He explicitly says "Father" but not Eli or Eloi, so how is it possible that the last and the most important three words by Jesus could be quoted so differently? The story of Jesus Christ's death has been narrated in four different ways in the four Gospels. According to Saint John's Gospel which is the last Gospel, there is no mention of Jesus Christ's crying out as it has been mentioned in other three Gospels.

John's Gospel

Chapter 19

Verse 28: After this, Jesus knowing that all things were now accomplished, that the scripture might be fulfilled, saith I thirst.

Verse 29: Now there was set a vessel full of vinegar: and they filled a spunge with vinegar, and put *it* upon hyssop, and put *it* to his mouth.

Verse 30: When Jesus therefore had received vinegar, he said, It is finished: and he bowed his head, and gave up the ghost.

Therefore, it is obviously seen that Jesus dies without crying out.

In general, the difference between all Gospels in relation to Jesus' death is as follows:

Mathew's Gospel: cries out loudly "Eli, Eli"

Mark's Gospel: cries out loudly "Eloi, Eloi"

Luke's Gospel: cries out loudly "father"

John's Gospel: he said, It is finished: and he bowed his head, and gave up the ghost.

Investigating the Old and New Testament as well as the religions and folks, which are in relation to them, is a huge task and I can't continue to do it due to a lack of time.

However, I shall shed the light on the essentials. Other scholars can follow and develop these points and do their contributions for further clarification of these points.

Following are only some of the contradictions extracted from the New Testament to open the way for other scholars' research.

Some problems and contradictions in the New Testament

In order to understand some of the sentences and words in the New (and Old) Testaments, two things are necessary:

> Familiarity with religion, history, ideas, traditions and even the language of the people that lived in that region, especially Mandaeans.

> Familiarity with Gnostic, Manda, Gnosticism, as well as Gnostic and Mandaean literature.

Otherwise those interpretations and readings made from the New and Old Testaments would only be baseless estimations.

First point:

Mathew's Gospel

Chapter 5

Verse 17: Think not that I am come to destroy the law, or the prophets: I am not come to destroy, but to fulfill.

These are the quotations from Jesus Christ, which are narrated in Matthew's Gospel, and it is one of the rare occasions where a word is repeated two times in the same verse. This repetition is indicating the emphasis. However, as it was illustrated earlier in this naration, Jesus Christ either changed or abolished some of the significant and basic laws of Jews, the Old Testament, and Holy Scriptures. These laws used to comprise the basis of Jewish faith and still continue to do so. For instance laws like circumcision, prohibition of divorce, baptism, violating the sacredness of the Sabbath (which is of high profanity for Jews and violating it would result in the death penalty). A group of Jews argued with Jesus Christ on some issues to show that his views opposed Judaism, for instance stoning the prostitutes.

It seems that those groups of Jews who opposed Jesus and challenged him with such questions remained as Jews, but the rest of them converted to Christianity.

Second point:

Matthew's Gospel and Luke's Gospel give different information about Joseph's generation tree. In Mathew's Gospel; chapter 1, verse 1, it begins with Abraham and comes to Joseph in verse 16, but in Luke's Gospel, which begins from chapter 3, verse 24, starts with Joseph and comes to Adam.

In Matthew's Gospel, which starts from Jacob, that is Joseph's (Mary's husband) father. In this Gospel, the generation tree comes to Solomon after David. From this point on, the difference between Matthew's Gospel and Luke's Gospel becomes obvious. In Luke's Gospel,

Joseph's father is Mat´that the son of Levi and continues to Mat´ta-tha the son of David.

<u>Saint Mathew's Gospel:</u>

Chapter 1

Verse 6: And Jesse begat David the King and David the King begat Solomon of her *that had been the wife of* U-ri´as.

Verse 7: And Solomon begat Ro-bo´am; and Ro-bo´am begat Abi´a, and Abi´a begat Asa.

Verse 8: And Asa begat Jos´a-phat, and Jos´a-phat begat Joram begat Ozi´as;

Verse 9: And Ozi´as begat Jo´a-tham; and Jo´a-tham begat A´chaz; and A´chaz begat Ez –e-ki´as;

Verse 10: And Ez-e-ki´as begat Ma-nas´ses; and Ma-nas´ses begat A´mon; and A´mon begat Jo-si´as;

Verse 11: And Jo-si´as begat Jech-o-ni´as and his brethren, about the time they were carried away to Babylon.

Verse 12: And after they were brought to Babylon, Jech-o-ni´as begat Sal-la´thi-el; and Sal-la´thi-el begat Zo-rob´a-bel.

Verse 13: And Zo-rob´a-bel begat A-bi´ud begat E-li´ud begat E-li´a-kim begat Azor,

Verse 14: And Azor begat Sa´doc; and Sa doc begat

A ́chim; and A ́chim begat Eli ́ud;

Verse 15: And E-li ́ud begat E-le-ázar and E-le-ázar begat Mat ́than and Mat ́than begat Jacob.

Verse 16: And Jacob begat Joseph the husband of Mary of whom was born Jesus, who is called Christ.

On the contrary, Luke's Gospel starts from Joseph and comes to Adam. In order to be economic, only the verses which reveal the difference are mentioned, as below:

<u>Saint Luke's Gospel</u>

Chapter 3

Verse 23: And Jesus himself began to be about thirty years of age, being (as was supposed) the son of Joseph, which was *the son* of He ́li.

Verse 24: Which was the son of Mat ́ that, which was *the son* of Levi, which was *the son* of Mel ́chi, which was *the son* of Joseph.

Verse 25: Which was *the son* of Mat- ta- thi ́as, which was *the son* of Amos, which was *the son* of Na ́um, which was *the son* of Es ́li, which was *the son* of Nag ́ge,

Verse 26: Which was *the son* of Ma ́ath, which was the son of Mat-ta-thías, which was *the son* of Sem ́e-I, which was *the son* of Juda,

Verse 27: Which was *the son* of Jo-an ́ na, which was

the son of Rhe'sa, which was *the son* of Zo-rob'a-bel, which was *the son* of Sa-la'thi-el which was *the son of* Ne'ri.

Verse 28: Which was *the son* of Mel'chi, which was *the son* of Ad'di, which was *the son* of Co'sam, which was *the son* of Er.

Verse 29: Which was *the son* of Jóse which was the son of E-li-e'zer, which was *the son* of Jo'rim, which was *the son* of Levi.

Verse 30: Which was the son of Simeon, which was *the son* of Jo'nan, which was *the son* of E-li'a-kim.

Verse 31: Which was *the son* of Me'le-a, which was *the son* of Me'nan, which was *the son* of Mat'ta-tha, which was the son of David.

The rest of the generation tree is similar to what has been mentioned in Matthew's Gospel.

If we accept that the generation tree mentioned in both Gospels belong to Mary's husband, Joseph, we can obviously see a contradiction concerning almost half of the generation tree mentioned in these two Gospels. Even the name of Joseph's father is mentioned differently in both Gospels. In Saint Matthew's Gospel his father's name is Jacob but in Luke's Gospel, his name is He'li.

Note:

The name He'li is written in different ways in different languages. This illustrates that in order to understand the meaning of the name (see Eli and Eloi); the Arabic version is more reliable because the variation in written form in Latin alphabet is confusing.

Persian and Arabic: Hali

هالى

Swedish:

Eli (which is very similar to the same Eli mentioned in Saint Matthew's Gospel, and is uttered by Jesus when he passes away)

English

He′li

German:

Elis (the German version is similar to Eli and Eloi mentioned in Matthew and Mark's Gospel but along with an additional /s/ at its end.

French:

De Heli

There is an interesting point in Luke's Gospel and that mentions the phrase:

Chapter 3

Verse 23: And Jesus himself began to be about thirty years of age, being (as was supposed) the son of Joseph, which was *the son* of He′li.

حسب گمان خلق پسر یوسف بن هالی

This considers Jesus Christ as Joseph's son and not God's son. This means that people believed in his being the son of Joseph, not God.

But if the duality observed in the generation means that there were two Josephs, then it is difficult to decide which one of them was Jesus Christ's step father or Mary's husband because this duality means two different people but with the same name - Joseph.

The fact that Joseph's generation tree is so confusing could be considered strong evidence to support its being fake. How could it be possible for them to know the name of Joseph's ancestors when they even did not know his father's name for sure while temporally speaking? His father was closer to Joseph than his forefathers. This is further evidence to support the inauthenticity of this generation tree; compressing the history of two centuries in 20 generations.

The conclusion is that even Joseph himself was not a Jew.

Note:

Jesus Christ passed away and ascended to heaven when he was 30 but his mother and his step father Joseph were still alive, his sister, brothers and apostles who lived long after him could have explained Joseph's generation tree to others and particularly their new fellow believers. But what is the reason for so much contradiction over such a short period of time? Could it not be evidence for the falseness of the whole story?

Third point

Matthew's Gospel

Chapter 15

From verse 24 on,   Israelites are likened to sheep and non-Israelite people are likened to worthless dogs who don't deserve anything.

The story started from the verse 22 where a Canaanite woman asked Jesus Christ to heal her sick daughter, but Jesus Christ did not even answer her until some of his followers reacted.

Verse 23: But he answered her not a word. And his disciples came and besought him, saying, Send her away; for she crieth after us.

Verse 24: But he answered and said, I am not sent but unto the lost sheep of the house of Israel.

Verse 25: Then came she and worshiped him, saying, Lord, help me.

Verse 26: But he answered and said, It is not meet to take children's bread, and to cast *it* to dogs.

Verse 27: And she said, Truth, Lord: yet the dogs eat of the crumbs which fall from their master's table.

Verse 28: then Jesus answered and said unto her, O

woman, great *is* thy faith: be it unto thee even as thou wilt. And her daughter was made whole from that very hour.

Here it becomes clear that Jesus Christ did not introduce himself as responsible for saving all of humanity, rather only the sheep of Israel; doing nothing for others who were worthless dogs.

In this case, we should again pay attention to the principal reason that most of the authors of the Bible (who were Jews) fabricated these stories. According to their view it was only Jews who were good people and the rest of the people on the earth were worthless dogs.

Nevertheless, based on this reasoning, he cannot be the great Lord (creator of the whole universe) or even the Son of the great Lord because his realm of authority is very limited. He is just a small local God.

While he looked upon the people around him in such a way, insulted them, and despised them, what would have been his reaction to the people who came from Africa or East Asia? The answer would be disappointing until and unless we accept that, all these delay were made by Jews to boost themselves even if its price was to defame Jesus Christ (the Lord or Lord's son), or that they lived in such a small world and never imagined that those simple words might someday be considered as sacred for billions of people. Of course, this is the most optimistic justification; otherwise one could think of a third alternative, and that is their intention was to deceive.

It should be noted that contrary to this assertion of the

New Testament, Mohammed, the prophet of Muslims, talks about the racial equality and introduces his faith to the whole world.

In order to support the above-mentioned story, a complementary quotation is mentioned:

Saint Mathew's Gospel

Chapter 10

Verse 5: These twelve Jesus sent forth, and commanded them, saying, go not into the way of the Gentiles, and into *any* city of the Sa-mar´i-tans enter ye not:

Verse 6: But go rather to the lost sheep of the house of Israel.

Verse 7 : And as ye go, preach, saying, the kingdom of heaven is at hand.

Verse 8: Heal the sick, cleanse the lepers, raise the dead, cast out devils: freely ye have received, freely give.

According to these verses, Jesus Christ sent 12 apostles to heal only the Israelites through the power he had bestowed upon them through miracle; however, they were not permitted to apply their power to help non-Israelites. This means Jesus Christ's philanthropy was just meant for Israelites and did not have a global realm at all. They were not supposed to think about their neighbors, let alone people from farther places. In the present world, such an attitude is considered racism and an offense in Europe. Even Jews' approach towards the Sabbath (not healing the sick people) is considered as offensive nowadays.

Here we can again conclude that Jews fabricated this story and naturally, their scope of thinking and acting did not cross their borders.

Fourth point

Saint Mathew's Gospel

Chapter 10

Verse 34: think not that I am come to send peace on earth: I came not to send peace, but a sword.

Verse 35: For I am come to set a man at variance against his father, and the daughter against her mother, and the daughter in law against her mother.

Verse 36: And a man's foes *shall be* they of his own household.

Verse 37: He that loveth father or mother more than me is not worthy of me: and he that loveth son or daughter more than me is not worthy of me.

Verse 38: And he that taketh not his cross and followeth after me, is not worthy of me.

Verse 39: He that findeth his life shall lose it: and he that loseth his life for my sake shall find it.

Verse 40: He that recieveth you receiveth me, and he that recevieth me recevieth him that sent me.

Verse 41: He that recevieth a prophet in the name of

prophet shall receive a prophet's reward; and he that recevieth a righteous man the name of a righteous man shall receive a righteous man's reward.

Verse 42: And whosoever shall give to drink unto one of these little ones a cup of cold *water* only in the name of a disciple, verily I say unto, he shall in no wise lose his reward.

Here in these verses Jesus Christ appeared as a warrior who separated the people from each other and ordered that they should have forgotten about their nearest people for his sake. He announced a kind of Jihad and named the ones killed on his way as martyrs and promised them with the reward of going to heaven. The same story today is going on among Muslims and considers martyrdom as going to haven.

It is hard to believe that these words might have had any relationship with peaceful Mandaean people. In addition, Mandaeans were ethnically and religiously a closed community who did not need to let the others among them. Moreover, all Mandaeans have always had one religion and such ideas, which have Jewish roots, have never existed among them.

As it is seen, in this verse the same sentence has been surprisingly repeated twice which is indicative of emphasis. In order to clarify the exact meaning of "peace", I will mention the different words used for this term in the Bible in different languages.

Persian: salamati/ سلامتى   صـــلح

Arabic: salaman/ سلامأ

English: Peace

Swedish: Fred

German: Friden

The term salamati/ سلامتی in bible means "peace" in these languages. It should be noted that salamati/ سلامتی which has been adopted in Persian translation of bible, is basically an Arabic word which means "peace". The word "سلام" /salam/ is also derived from the same word. So, Jesus Christ explicitly said that he had not come for peace and had the intention to start a war; a war with those who were not accompanying him. Of course, the above-mentioned argument should be interpreted with regard to other issues too, which have been mentioned before. This means that logically, as Jesus was sent only for Israelite sheep, his sword too must have been meant only for them.

Jesus Christ's mission was not universal and his retribution was not meant for all human beings.

Jesus Christ was not aware of the existence of lands like Iran, China, Japan, America, Australia, etc and this unawareness was unlike the God who created the whole universe. If a God were not aware of the Lands and the people he has created how would it be possible for this God to be aware of the events going on in a universe which is 14 billion light-years away?

In fact, it seems that Jesus Christ's story is a domestic conflict or battle among Jews themselves. Those Jews who converted to Christianity threatened other Jews with death in case they would not have converted too.

Further interpretations of this book take more time and the present brief interpretation suffices to be the key for opening the doors and ways for having a correct and reasonable interpretation.

I hope this writing would help Christians to throw off the shackles that Jews have put on them and not to see themselves as obliged to publish the Old Testament along with New Testament and bow before the murderers of the messenger that they believe in him and in his story.

-By taking into consideration this important issue (the non-Jewish origin of Jesus Christ and his mother); Christians should throw away the shackles that Jews have put on them and stop to have a different look.

-Christians should start fighting against the Zionist churches.

-Instead of Old Testament, Christians should publish the Mandaean books like Ginza Rba.

-Christians should be aware of the major difference between Old Testament and Mandaean books; that Old Testament is full of violence and massacre in various ways while Mandaean scriptures talk about peace, and brotherhood.

<u>Saint John's Gospel is a Mandaean Gospel</u>

In this piece of writing, some of the contradictions observed in the four Gospels were mentioned. It is now time to put forward the main point of the contradictions among Gospels. There used to be multiple numbers of Gospels but the church restricted them to four Gospels and tried to destroy the others. In 1945, a crock was found in Nag Jammadi in Egypt. According to researchers, the Gospels, which were buried in this crock, were hidden in this way to be protected against destruction . Nevertheless, one can argue that some of these Gospels were Gnostic or Mandaean.

<u>One of the important and challenging questions is the question of creation of the Universe and the important role of the "Word":</u>

According to "Ginza Rba", God has created the whole world with "Word" which is the manifestation of God's will and order. It seems that the meaning of "word" is God's will and providence. God is the creator of the whole universe and the creator of all beauties and all have been created according to his order. Moving clouds, running waters, tall trees, animals and the light, which exists in the world, all have received their life from "Hayyi". Hayyi is the creator of the world of light, and is superior to all angels and is their creator." (Ginza Rba, quoted from Sabeine Rastin, p, 76).

The point that God's will or even God himself has been interpreted as "word" is an important issue in the debate of Genesis. That is why some say: God said: be! and, whatever exists began to be created. This is contrary to the Jewish story of six days of creation because word does not contain time but six days of creation is a long time, moreover one should take rest one day.

Coincidentally, Saint John's Gospel begins with "word":

<u>Saint John's Gospel:</u>

Chapter 1

Verse 1: In the beginning was the Word, and the Word was with God.

Verse 2: The same was in the beginning with God.

Verse 3: All things were made by him, and without his was not anything made that was made.

Verse 4: In him was life; and the life was the light of men.

Verse 5: And the light shineth in darkness; and the darkness comprehended it not.

Verse 6: There was a man sent from God, whose name was John.

Verse 7: The same came for a witness, to bear witness of the light, that all *men* through him might believe.

Verse 8: He was not that light, but *was sent* to beat witness of that Light.

Verse 9: *That* was the true Light, which lighteth every man that cometh into the world.

Verse 10: He was in the world, and the world was made by him, and the world knew him not.

Verse 11: He came unto his own, and his own received him not.

Verse 12: But as many as received him, to him gave he power to become the sons of God, *even* to them that believe on his name;

Verse 13: Which were born, not to blood, nor of the will of the flesh, nor of the will of man, but of God.

Verse 14: And the Word was made flesh, and dwelt among us, (and we beheld his glory, the glory as of the only begotten of the Father) full of grace and truth.

Verse 15: John bare witness of him, and cried, saying, This was he of whom I spake, He that cometh after me is preferred before me; for he was before me.

 At the beginning, there is a mention of "word" that God has willed and said "be" and all the world and universe were created in a moment.

The Big bang theory, which was proposed by the Belgian priest George Lemaitre in 1930, was based on this idea. Even the creation of the world by "word" sounds more reasonable in comparison to the six-day Genesis story, which does not sound to be a reasonable explanation nowadays.

It seems that the theory of creating the universe by "word" is the same in both Saint John's Gospel and Mandaeans' Ginza Rba, but it is not compatible with the

Jews theory of Genesis mentioned in Old Testament. It seems that the story of Genesis in 6 days has been borrowed from Iranians and the book of Genesis is the last book which has been written, and that the whole Old Testament was written during the Achaemenid Empire (2500 years ago) with their financial support. The reasons for this claim are the books of Ezra, Nehemiah and Esther, which are entirely Iranians' stories.

According to the experts, these verses in John's Gospel are the best manifestations of Mandaean (Gnosis) literature.

Mandaeans believe that the greatest gift that God has bestowed on humans is knowledge. Knowledge brightens the heart. Man should not believe in a partner for God because God has given him wisdom and one can get help from this wisdom.

Mandaeans also believe in hereafter. In the left part of Ginza Rba it is written: this world will be extinct and your deeds will leave you. Do not worship the devil idols and the appearance of this world. Those who worship the devil will be in pain and fire till the day of resurrection. Mandaeans call the heaven as Almadenhura and hell as Almadehshukha.

<u>Mysticism, Gnosis, Manda</u>

What is a common point among Iranian and Islamic Mysticism, Gnosis in Greece and Manda among Canaanites, is the belief in duality of God on the one hand and the idea of reaching to God on the other hand. In ancient Greece, there existed many Gods until they also began to change under the influence of Mandaeans. Plotinus (204-270) systematized the Greek Gnosis and it became known as Neoplatonism. According to the Plotinus' biography, it can be inferred that **Greek Gnosis is adopted from Canaanites' Manda**.

Jews were living in turmoil. Everyone had a God for him or herself so that sometimes they used to carry their God under their clothes until the time of Joshua's reign. In order to unite the people for attacking Canaan, he ordered the people to believe in only one God, namely; Yahweh, otherwise they would be killed. (For further information you can see my site where I have developed this issue). Even during Joshua's time, monotheism was not established completely and duality seemed to be more suitable at that time. In fact, Yahweh is the God of Evil and is very different from the Mighty God who has created the universes.

Ultimately, under the influence of Canaanites' Manda, Jews also adopted Mandaean literature.

To deem Jesus as God or God's son is a Mandaean (mystic or Gnostic) literature. That some people believed in duality was common at that time which is indicative of the fact that in that period some Jews had just begun to believe in duality. They did not change the Old Testament but they embarked on making new readings from it and, in doing so, they advanced so far that they became blind to it and made the others believe them blindly as well. The fact is that the Old Testament is a long path from thousand-theism (where everyone had a God for him or herself) to polytheism (confusing and unknown).

The Old Testament cannot be considered precisely and decisively as a book advocating only one God.

Mandaean, Gnosis or Mystic literature is based on duality and is not compatible with monotheism, because in monotheism reaching to God and becoming God is profanity. That is why Islam banned this thinking; nevertheless, the vigor of the remaining culture left its influence and mysticism emerged, but it took many centuries for it to open its way among Shiites. Mohammad, the prophet of Muslims, ascended to heaven only once and he could just see a light of God not God itself. It is quite clear that mentioning this point bears significance in two ways; satisfying the public opinion, and from a religious point of view. However, neither Mohammad nor any of his relatives had a claim about being God and they took that as profanity. Therefore, according to Muslims, even if there is someone who should get to God or be God, it is in the first place Mohammad and then Caliphates. In the early years of Islam's advent some people represented Ali (Mohammad's son in-law and fourth caliphate) as an image of God. It is famous that such a claim was made by Abdullah bin Saba, a newly converted Jew to

Islam. Later some people made God out of some other people or they themselves claimed to be God. In Iran there were many people who claimed to be like Jesus.

In Iran a Shiate Seyyed known as Seyyed Ali Mohammad Shirazi (1819-1859- killed) claimed to be the Baab (door) for which he was judged and sentenced to death. To be Baab has also been attributed to Jesus in Bible. Later his heir, titled Baha allah (1817-1892) claimed to be

من يظهر الله و موعود

(the chosen one) and even being God . He was banished to Palestine, which was ruled by the Ottoman Empire and died in Acre. Mansour Hallaj (killed in 922 AD-309 AH) in Iran claimed that he was God and was brutally murdered but he never moaned in pain under an executioner's hand (similar to Jesus in Mark's and Mathew's Gospel) that is why his story has remained among Iranians as an extraordinary example of resistance. Some other people also claimed being God.

The fact that we are a part of God or God itself or not has been a natural part of our thought and philosophical arguments so that: in case we are not a part of God, there is a kind of duality where on the one hand there is God and on the other hand there is us and the universe. Otherwise all is one.

one was, he was not only one:

یکی بود، یکی نبود

We are a part of God and consequently God. The way

to reach to the stage where one can call himself God is Mysticism and revelation.

<u>Miracles and "Keramat" کرامــات</u>

The miracles have existed before duality:

If someone had done something trivial, it was exaggerated as much as possible. Miracles have happened all over the world and as William Durant says; if someone talks about the Jesus' miracles to a Hindu, she/he might answer: did he only do these simple things? Our smallest God was capable of doing miracles bigger than that! Nevertheless, Miracles are the product of duality or polytheistic ideas. However when Mohammad the Prophet of Muslims stepped forward, he was not able to claim performing any miracles for two reasons: first, he wanted to introduce one God and second, it was no longer possible to cheat and lie under the term 'miracle'.

Miracles happen when and among those who have at least two Gods and want to unite with one of them, as it is in the case of Mysticism, Gnosism and Mandaeism.

Contrary to his forerunners, Mohammad never claimed to have performed a miracle. However, shortly after him, mystic ideas inserted into Islam and even some people claimed to be God and to prove it, they performed some miracles, which they called "keramat" کرامــات

 However, the basis for Jesus Christ's miracles is so

shaky that there is no reason left to call them miracles. For instance:

Mathew's Gospel

Chapter 8

Verse 23: And when he was entered into a ship, his disciples followed him.

Verse 24: And behold, there arose a great tempest in the sea, insomuch that the ship was covered with waves: but he was asleep.

Verse 25: And his disciples came to *him*, and awoke him, saying, Lord, save us; we perish.

Verse 26: And he saith unto the, Why are ye fearful, Oye of little faith? Then he arose, and rebuked the winds and the sea; and there was a great calm.

Verse 27: But the man marveled, saying, what manner of man is this, that even the winds and the sea obey him!

Verse 28: And when he was come to the other side into the country of Ger′ge-sense, there met him two possessed with devils, coming out of the tombs, exceeding fierce, so that no man might pass by that way.

This story sounds to be fake and fabricated because the sea they are talking about is the little lake known as the Sea of Galilee. It is clearly mentioned that it was on the other side of the land known as Gergistan جرجیستان

This lake is almost triangular and it covered an area of about 166 sq. km; it is many hundred meters below the sea level and it is surrounded by mountains. The Sea of Galilee is a very small lake and the possibility of having such a storm in there is non existent and would be like a storm in a cup. Interestingly some of the disciples of Jesus Christ could swim and the story is not supportable because it is completely fake and fabricated and there remains no place for such a storm and consequently such a miracle. Similar to this story, most of the other stories of miracles can be investigated and rejected.

Miracles were not and are not only limited to Jesus Christ but to hundreds or perhaps thousands who used to do miracles and still do today. As a result, the miracles, which are attributed to Jesus Christ, cannot be the evidence for his rightfulness. On the contrary, he should have given exact instructions for running the society, which he did not do at all.

If we take these miracles as the reason for his being God, or the son of God, then we should admit that hundreds or thousands of people (who have performed miracles better than Jesus' miracles) are and will be God or God's sons. One of the differences between religion and philosophy is the superiority of religious instructions to logical instructions. But Jesus Christ does not even provide his followers with appropriate religious instructions.

Miracles and Keramat کرامات have no compatibility with reason, logic, and realities. Rather they are some claims and deceptions for influencing common people in order to abuse them.

Hayyi, the greatest God

The most supreme being in Mandaean faith and their only God is Hayyi. Hayyi is an indefinite God whose power is not comparable with anything else. According to Mandaean faith, Hayyi means "life and living". This word is in fact in plural form and the purpose of using it in plural form is to show respect and to add to its mysteriousness. God's name in Mandaean faith is also associated with رب /rab/ which means great. Great God, high God, or supreme God.

Contrary to other Gods that become angry, judge, and interfere in history, Hayyi is so Great that he does not interfere in such things directly. God in Mandaean faith is eternal and nothing existed prior to it. He is true and everlasting. It is not seen and it has no boundary. It is not subject to evolution. No one is like him and his light has filled the whole world. He has no father and no one can dominate him. He is the absolute ruler and his might is not to be shared with anyone. All stars and planets are created by him. Whoever worships some other God than him or worships him in a temple which is not built for him is sentenced to be placed in a dark mountain (a place like hell). (a part of Ginza Rba).

The story of Eve and Adam among Mandaean

According to Mandaean scriptures, Adam is the first human and is the father of Mandaean. According to Mandaean tradition, the history of the creation of human dates back to 445000 years ago. This is contrary to Jews who consider this date to be 8960 years.

Eve and Adam had three sons called Abel, Seth (same as شیث in Arabic,) Enosh, and a daughter. Since according to Mandaean faith marriage of sisters and brothers was prohibited, therefore by God's order, 60 Ether or non-physical beings along with their families were sent from the realm of light known as Kušta in order to marry Adam's children. Thus, the base stone of human community was created out of the marriage of human and these Ethers.

It is interesting to note that among Muslims, the question that has always been raised is if God created only one couple, then their children were siblings and marriage among them was forbidden, even if it was not prohibited at the beginning (it became prohibited later). The question is then why did God not try to solve this problem from the beginning and did not create some more couples like Eve and Adam?

Nevertheless, it is seen that the legend or fabricated creation story among Muslims and Jews are almost the same but it differs from Mandaean version of the Genesis story.

This story has not been discussed among Christians but in John's Gospel there is a mention of the "word" which is a new discussion about and more modern view towards the creation of the universe.

It is not clear why those Jews who converted to Christianity did not pay attention to this point despite the plethora of things they had borrowed from Mandaeanim.

According to the accounts by Ginza Rba (the Great

treasure), which is Mandaean's holy book, human society has left several stages behind until it has come to great stage of Noah's storm, which is the period that we are in now.

Noah and Noah's storm story is Mandaean

The only difference between Noah's period and periods prior to it is that at the end of previous periods, only one couple was left but in the next periods, there remained more than one couple. In this period, in addition to Noah and his wife Anhuraita, their son Shem (sem) and his wife Noritha remained. Noah's name among Mandaean is Neo.

When the ship set off, Shem was left behind but succeeded to reach to the ship's roof and during the eleven months that the storm was raging, he was fed by Hibel-Ziwa who is the same as Gabriel. Mandaeans believe that Shem and his wife Noritha نوريثا were their progenitors. Jews also consider Shem (sem) as their ancestor. It is interesting to know that Jews consider themselves as the only Semitic people. Their racist (dangerous word to use) motivation for coining the term anti-Semitism is to suppress their opponents, while the fact of the matter is that today most of the Jews have non-Semitic origins.

The Noah's storm legend continued by Ruha's (the queen of darkness) appearance to Noah in the image of Noah's wife namely Anhuraita and her fornicating with him. The result was the birth of Ham (progenitor of black people), Yam, progenitor of white people,

Abraham and Jews, and Yafet the progenitor of Gipsy/Romans.

According to the settlement areas of Mandaean people, Noah's storm must have happened in their areas and it is a Mandaean story. Such an event could not have happened for the Nomad Arabs (Jews). However, Mandaeans have always been lowlanders and they have frequently seen such events.

Significance of Sabbath for Jews

Saturday is the holiday for Jews so that no one is allowed to work. The punishment for working in Sabbath, even plucking wheat is heavy, even stoning.

Mathew's Gospel

Chapter 12

Verse 1: At that time Jesus went on the Sabbath day through the corn; and his disciples were an hungred, and began to pluck the ears of corn, and to eat.

Verse2: But when the Pharisees saw *it*, they said unto him, behold, thy disciples do that which is not lawful to do upon the Sabbath day.

According to these verses, it is inferred that even plucking wheat and eating it at the same time for quenching your hunger is considered work. During Sabbath, Jews just must lie down and do nothing. In John's Gospel, Jesus Christ was criticized many times for working on Sabbath. Even his healing an ill person was considered disgusting and made him deserve death.

John's Gospel

Chapter 5

Verse 15: The man departed and told the Jews that it was Jesus which had made him whole.

Verse 16: And therefore did the Jews prosecute Jesus, and sought to slay him, because he had done these things on the Sabbath day.

Verse 17: But Jesus answered them, My Father worketh hitherto, and I work.

Verse 18: Therefore the Jews sought the more to kill him, because he not only had broken the Sabbath, but said also that God was his father, making him equal with God.

For further information and understanding the problems of Sabbath where even midwives were not allowed to work and people used to face several problems- you can refer to the sources compiled in recent years. One of them is "the weight of three thousand years" written by Israel Shahak, a professor of Polish origin who lives in Israel.

In order to shed further light on the harshness of the punishments for working on Sabbath, below are some old Testament verses from the five books of Moses or Torah which are the most important parts of it and they are attributed to Moses.

Book of Exodus

Chapter 31

Verse 12: And the LORD spake unto Moses, saying,

Verse 13: Speak thou also unto the children of Israel, saying, Verily my Sabbaths ye shall keep: for it is a sign between me and you throughout your generations, that ye may know that I am the LORD that doth sanctify you.

Verse 14: Ye shall keep the Sabbath therefore, for it is only you: every one that defileth it shall surly be put to death: for whosoever doeth any work therein, that soul shall be cut off from among his people.

Verse 15: six days may work be done, but in the seventh is the Sabbath of rest, holy to the LORD: whosoever doeth any work in the Sabbath day, he shall surely be put to death.

In these verses, the ones who violate Sabbath day are openly sentenced to death.

Chapter 35

Verse 1: And Moses gathered all the congregation of the children of Israel together, and said unto them. These are the words ye should do them.

Verse 2 : Six days shall work be done, but on the seventh day there shall be to you an holy day, a Sabbath of rest to the LORD: whosoever doeth work therein shall be out to death.

Verse 3: Ye shall kindle no fire throughout your habitation upon the Sabbath day.

In these verses, the order for killing the people violating the Sabbath is issued. Even where it is mentioned that people should avoid making fire at their homes for making food, it is looked upon as working and violating the Sabbath whose punishment is a death penalty.

In order to find out the religious tricks that modern Jews use to work on Sabbath, (for instance usury in banks), you can refer to the same book "the weight of three thousand years" written by Israel Shahak the Polish professor.

The Book of Numbers

Chapter 15

Verse 32: And while the children of Israel were in the wilderness, they found a man that gathered sticks upon the Sabbath day.

Verse 33: And they that found him gathering sticks brought him unto Moses and Aaron, and unto all the congregation.

Verse 34: And they put him in ward, because it was not declared what should be done to him.

Verse 35: And the LORD said unto Moses, The man shall be surely put to death: all the congregation shall stone him with stones without the camp.

Verse 36: And all the congregation brought him without the camp, and stoned him with stones, and he died; as the LORD commanded Moses.

So it is observed how a poor man whose only income source was gathering firewood was brutally stoned and killed with no mercy towards him and his family. Those who gathered firewood were the poorest people of that time who did not have even a square meter on earth or even a goat.

Note: considering Saturday as holiday in the West was under the pressure of Jews.

Sunday as holiday; a Mandaean tradition

Mandaean people believe that John hid until he was 22 years old in order to protect his life from the Jews. Then his hiding period came to an end by Lord's order and he appeared in Jerusalem. On a Sunday in Jerusalem, a voice was heard that said a great man was about to come. "a messenger has come to Jerusalem whose nose and mouth seems like Nishbai, and his body features are like her husband Zacharya. Nishbai left the house in worry and anxiety running towards the owner of voice. When she looked at the 22-year-old young man, she realized that he was her own lost and hidden child, John. She hugged him, as her waiting came to an end and finally found her child".

John's appearance on a Sunday after 22 years of hiding makes Sundays to be of significance for Mandaeans. In addition, the hostility among the Mandaeans and Jews did not allow them to welcome each others' holidays; rather they illustrated antipathy. As a result, when Jews converted to this new religion, they tried to keep their holidays distinct from the Jewish holiday in order to show that they have completely separated themselves from their previous religion. The same holds true for Muslims who have selected Friday as their holiday.

John was not interested in getting married until there came a heavenly voice. "Thou, John, get married and let your longing come to tranquility. Pray your God on Sundays and Thursdays and avoid anything in the void world".

By getting the Lord's command, John got married and had some children. Sundays and Thursdays were selected for saying prayers, and Sunday was of more significance.

Mandaeans accepted Sunday as the day for saying prayers and do other jobs and this tradition was transferred to Christians in order to set themselves free from the violence and strict rules of Sabbath and its punishments. Mandaeans who used to have Sundays as holiday, in no way could have been the same as Jews who used to have Sabbath (Saturday as holiday). For Jews, working on Saturdays (Sabbath) had the death punishment, therefore in case Mandaeans were also Jews, they should have had Saturday as their holiday.

Some examples of stoning and brutality in the Old Testament

Book of Genesis:

Chapter 34: Jacob entered the Shechem in Canaan. The prince of the country fell in love with Jacob's daughter and laid with her. The prince and his father went to Jacob and asked for his daughter for marriage and offered them land and many reasonable coffers and promises. However, Jacob and his sons used a trick and told them they would accept only if all males from child to old man be circumcised. The next day after circumcision when all were in bed in pain, Jacob and his sons attacked them with swords, killed all males from child to old, took their women as captive, plundered their properties, and ran away.

The entire chapter is dealing with this story, which is an evidence of the massacre of Canaanites by these merciless and aggressive people. This story is another reason for the historical hatred of Israelites by the Canaanites. This is probably the reason for the Israelites' (or Jacob's clan who was called Israel after wrestling with God) exodus to Egypt. It must have been the same massacre they did in Canaan and they were afraid of its consequences. As Jacob said "we should run otherwise they will come and take revenge". After coming back from Egypt and killing the people of that region, the conquered lands were divided among twelve tribes. From among these twelve tribes, only two of them remained after the Babylonians pushed ten of those tribes eastward. The remaining two tribes were known as Jews.

Book of Deuteronomy

Chapter 21

Verse 19: Then shall his father and his mother lay hold on him, and bring him out unto the elders of his city, and unto the gate of his place;

Verse 20: And they shall say unto the elders of his city, this our son is stubborn and rebellious, he will not obey our voice; he is a glutton, and a drunkard.

Verse 21: And all the men of his city shall stone him to death with stones: so shalt thou put away the evil from the midst of thee; and all Israel shall hear, and fear.

In these verses it is recommended to stone the child in case they don't obey the parents, so that others get scared and obey their parents.

Book of Deuteronomy

Chapter 22

Verse 20: But if this thing be true, that the tokens of virginity were not found in the damsel;

Verse 21: then they shall bring out the damsel to the door of her father's house, and the men of her city shall stone her to death with stones, because she hath wrought folly in Israel, to play the harlot in her father's house: so shalt thou put away the evil from the midst of thee.

In these verses, the punishment for a girl who has a fiancé but commits adultery and becomes deflowered is being stoned. Based on these verses, if Mary and Joseph were Jews and Mary had become pregnant, she should have been stoned. The important point is that contrary to Greek people, Jews did not believe in marriage with God or God's child and could not accept at all that Mary was married to God and became pregnant. As a result, Mary should have been stoned which she was not; until and unless we accept that Mary and Joseph were not Jews.

Verse 22: If a man be found lying with a woman married to a husband, then they shall both of them die, the man that lay with the woman, and the woman: so shalt thou put away the evil from Israel.

In the following verses, it is explicitly mentioned that the punishment for a married woman who commits adultery is death.

Verse 23: If there be a damsel that is a virgin betrothed unto a husband, and a man find her in the city, and lie with her;

Verse 24: then ye shall bring them both out unto the gate of that city, and ye shall stone them to death with stones; the damsel, because she cried not, being in the city; and the man, because he hath humbled his neighbor's wife: so thou shalt put away the evil from the midst of thee.

According to these verses, the punishment for a sexual relationship (adultery) is death, especially for those like Mary who had a fiancé but had slept with someone else.

Joshua stepped to power after Moses and attacked Jericho, and destroyed the city but later he faced a problem and then came to the conclusion that someone called Achan had not handed him some of the properties and had taken them away to his tent. As a result, not only Achan himself, but also his children, cattle, tent and any living belonging within it were stoned to death.

Book of Joshua

Chapter 7

Verse 23: And they took them out of the midst of the tent, and brought them unto Joshua, and unto all the children of Israel, and laid them out before the LORD.

Verse 24: And Joshua, and all Israel with him, took Achan the son of Zerah, and the silver, and the garment, and the wedge of gold, and his sons, and his daughters, and his oxen, and his asses, and his sheep, and his tent, and all that he had: and they brought them unto the valley of Achor.

Verse 25: And Joshua said, Why hast thou troubled us? the LORD shall trouble thee this day. And all Israel stoned him with stones, and burned them with fire, after they had stoned them with stones.

Verse 26: And they raised over him a great heap of stones unto this day. So the LORD turned from the fierceness of his anger. Wherefore the name of that place was called, The Valley of Achor, unto this day.

A point which is inferred from this discussion is mentioning the word "tent" which is indicative of the fact that Jews had a nomadic life style and had no fixed houses. This means that they used to live in tents not in urban houses made of stone and brick.

There were some instances where they used to stone even the animals. An example is mentioned below:

Book of Exodus

Chapter 21

Verse 28 until 31of chapter 21 of Exodus is about stoning a cow; that is to say if a cow would gore a man and would kill him, the cow and in some cases its owner were stoned. It is clearly seen that stoning is a typical Jewish punishment and they used to stone not only the sinful person, but also all his relatives, innocent cattle, tent, carpet, bowl and pitcher.

There are some other violent instructions as well:

Book of Deuteronomy

Chapter 19

Verse 21: And thine eyes shall not pity; life shall go for life, eye for eye, tooth for tooth, hand for hand, foot for foot.

This is the same retribution as in Islam.

Book of Deuteronomy

Chapter 20

Verse 16: But of the cities of these peoples, which the LORD thy God doth give these for an inheritance, thou shalt save alive nothing that breatheth.

These verses are evidence of the massive massacre that the Israelites (Jews) committed in the region and the reason for why Mandaean people hate them. If we take into consideration the names of the people and tribes which are mentioned in these verses, it become obvious that they had killed innocent people on such a massive scale by the command of this merciless God, Yahweh, just in order to empty the region for the settlement of Jews. It seems that today, the same recipe is used in the case of occupied Palestine.

Verse 17:   But thou shalt utterly destroy them: the Hittites, and the Amorites, the Canaanites, and the Perizzites, the Hivites, and the Jebusites; as the LORD thy God hath commanded thee;

The collection of the punishments and strict rules of Judaism (only some of them were mentioned above) made the people look for or create a new religion which was simple, peaceful and had no such harsh rules. Therefore, inspired by the Mandaean rules, they made a new religion, which took many years to be formed, recognized and known as Christianity.

According to the geographical scope of Mandaeans' settlement, they were all Canaanites.

According to Mandaean sources, Mandaeans used to reside around Jerusalem and coastal areas of Jordan River. Linguists argue that the word "Yardena" (flowing water) is motivated by Palestine's environment and it seems that the names Jordan or Jordan River are also derived from the same root. In the beginning, Mandaeans used to call the Jordan river "Yardena" but later, they extended the term "Yardena" to refer to any flowing stream like Karun, Tigris, and Euphrates. "Ginza Rba" , "Book of Revelation" and "Haran Gawaita" emphasize on the sacredness of Jerusalem as a city which was built after Noah's storm. According to Ginza Rba, there were 360 messengers in Jerusalem who believed the same thing but then left the city. John, the last prophet of Mandaeans, was born in Jerusalem and used to baptize the people in the River Jordan. The reason of significance of Jerusalem in Mandaean text is its being the first and main settlement of Mandaeans. Contrary to Jews, Egyptians are not remarked upon extensively in Mandaean scriptures or verbal narratives. This can be due to the conflicts between Mandaeans and Jews.

Today, Iranian Mandaeans don't associate themselves with Egyptians; however, their negative view of Jews can illustrate their roots of thousand years of conflict with the Israelites.

A quotation from the book "Tamidiyan" means "Baptism":

"…What is undoubtedly inferred from Mandaean scriptures and modern Mandaeans' impression from their history is that they used to settle in Palestine and near Jerusalem. According to "Haran Gawaita" which is one of the holy Mandaean scriptures - and contain the history of Mandaean as well as some predictions about future - Mandaeans used to live in a city where "Jewish rulers" had no way in. Over them was King Ardban (Artabanus) who along with sixty thousand Našoraeans entered the "Median hills" a place where they were free from domination by all other folks".

<u>Some evidence from the Old Testament</u>

In chapter thirteen of the book of Numbers it is said that after Moses' Exodus from Egypt and their (the Israelites) arrival in Palestine, the Israelites put Moses under pressure due to poverty and hunger and started denying the Lord. Then Lord became angry and decided to punish them, but Moses told the Lord that if he would do so, Egyptians would Laugh at the Lord…….Therefore the Lord changed his mind.

<u>Interesting point is that the Lord himself was not wise enough to think about such issues and Moses gave him advice and guided him.</u>

In order to find some place to accommodate them, Moses sent some as spies to neighboring areas, in order to spot the location of the inhabitants of those areas.

Moses himself could not reside in any land but after him, Joshua made a brutal massacre in five Canaanite cities - that was not matched in human history- and occupied the lands which they later claimed to possess, then and even now.

Book of Numbers

Chapter 13

Verse 1: And the LORD spake unto Moses, saying,

Verse 2: Send thou men, that they may search the land of Canaan, which I give unto the children of Israel: of every tribe of their fathers shall ye send a man, every one a ruler among them.

The Lord promised Canaan to Moses and told him to send spies. So it become clear that in this religion "spying is divine and legal" or a "divine rule".

The names of the spies were revealed and they were sent on mission to provide a report from each region and introduce some of the lands, which were hard to occupy.

Verse 27: And they told him, and said, We came unto the land whither thou sentest us, and surely it floweth with milk and honey, and this is the fruit.

Note: In previous verses this fruit that they had cut with its branches is identified as grapes.

Verse 28: Nevertheless the people be strong that dwell in the land, and the cities are saw the children of Anak there.

Verse 29: The Amalekites dwell in the land of the south,

and the Hittites, and the Jebusites, and the Amorites, dwell in the mountains, and the Canaanites dwell by the sea, and by the coast of Jordan.

One can have several inferences from these verses: for instance, Jews had not seen grapes before and did not know how to break the fort. This is indicative of their being primitive and…

According to this information, Canaanites resided in an area between Jordan River, Jerusalem, and Dead Sea. This is the same area, which has been mentioned in Mandaean books because Mandaeans used to settle near water, and this region was the best area for their settlement as it was surrounded by water.

Similar to other people around the world who have an ancient background; Mandaeans had also reached peace and wisdom due to having old civilization and long years of settlement.

After long years in search for the answer to the question of creation and Genesis, they came up with the story of "good and evil" which is a duality. That is why they are considered as Gnostic and they left behind a thoroughly Gnostic and pure literature. That is why they have been called Mandaean, which is equal to "Gnostic" or "mystic".

It should be noted that even though both Jews and Mandaeans consider themselves as the heirs of Shem, in some ways, this is true for almost all the people of that region because even those who are called Arabs associate themselves with Shem. However, there are some differences among them.

First, according to Old Testament, Abraham's clan moved to this area from the south east areas that is south of Iraq, and entered the Canaan when they first crossed the Jordan River. On the contrary, Canaanites used to reside near the water since long back and the legend of Noah's storm belonged to these people, and Jews have borrowed this legend from Canaanites who later became known as Mandaean.

If we accept that there existed such a story and there were some people who were Shem's heirs, they should be these Canaanites (Mandaean) and Jews are not right in associating themselves with Shem. Most probably the early migration of Canaanites (Mandaean) to southern regions of Iran (Khuzestan) and Iraq was due to the massacre they went through by the Israelites (later known as Jews) not due to Nebuchadnezzar. Similar to their early migration, their second migration was also due to the massacre by the Jews after Jesus Christ's story.

Mandaeans were not despotic people in search of war, and that is why Nebuchadnezzar had no reason to move the people who were no threat to him. It seems that due to the pressures, plunders and massacres that Jews committed, Canaanites voluntary sought refuge from the Babylonian king.

No wise king, administration, or government evacuates its residents from a fertile land, especially if they are peaceful people who pose no threat. Such people can be the best economic support for any power by working, producing and paying taxes.

Moving a group of people en masse happened only when the people were warriors and adventurous, and therefore they were moved in order to get rid of them or to use them for suppressing other people. As a result, the theory of Mandaeans' forced migration to Iran and Iraq by Nebuchadnezzar does not sound reasonable.

Book of Numbers

Chapter 33

This chapter defines Moses' route, which ultimately ends up acrossed the land of Canaan. However, Israelites have no place to settle in. Moses' God tells him to occupy this land, and kill its residents because even if one of them survives, it will be like a thorn in their sides.

Verse 55: But if ye will not drive out the inhabitants of the land from before you; then it shall come to pass, that those which ye let remain of them shall be pricks in your eyes, and thorns in your sides, and shall vex you in the land wherein ye dwell.

happen, that those, which ye let remain of them, shall be pricks in your eyes, and thorns in your sides, and shall vex you in the land wherein ye dwell.

Verse 56: Moreover it shall come to pass, that I shall do unto you, as I thought to do unto them.

These thorns (Canaanites) are still surviving and the bells are ringing to put an end to these lies about history, Mandaeans and Jesus.

Investigating the name of Mandaean

Greek, Jewish and Christian Gnosis are borrowed from Canaanite Manda (Gnosis)

"Manda" means knowledge, or Gnosis, and is equivalent to the path of righteousness, Sufi and the like.

Thus it is observed that Mandaean is not a name derived from a land or ethnicity, rather it is an epithet or attribute which has been given to these people; that is the people of knowledge and gnosis. Mandaean is an epithet, which has been attributed to these people due to their wise and ascetic life style.

Manda is an attribute that is now known as the name of these people and it is not rooted in their ethnicity or nationality. A name which has its roots in nationality is mostly derived from the name of the land of residence or the name of the person who is known to be the first person of those people. Similarly they were called Canaanites before, which means that the people whose land is called Canaan. Today, these people prefer to be called as "Mandaean Sabia" which means that the people of "Baptist Gnosis".

As those people were not warriors, and had no interest in wealth and power either, it sufficed for them to find a place to live and some food to survive on. Most probably, these people's Manda existed before Greek Gnosis and affected the whole region including Greek Gnosis because Mandaeans and Greeks were neighbors.

On the same basis, Jews (nomad Arabs) who later

entered the region with Moses in such a way, were not the people of Gnosis or Manda. Most probably Jewish Gnosis is derived from Canaanites' Manda. Following the same rationale, the Christian Gnosis also has roots in Canaanite Gnosis (Mandaean Sabia).

Some points which define the Mandaean Gnosis:

Light versus Darkness

Heaven versus Earth (earth is materialistic and unclean but Heaven is clean and divine)

Clean versus Unclean

Creation versus Modification

Killing of Mandaeans (Canaanites) at the hands of the Israelites

Israelites (later known as Jews) massacred the Mandaeans (Canaanites) brutally and massively and this became the root and never-ending hatred of Mandaeans towards Jews.

Book of Deuteronomy

Chapter 34

Verse 1: And Moses went up from the plains of Moab unto the mountain of Nebo, to the top of Pisgah, that is over against Jericho. And the LORD shewed him all the land of Gilead, unto Dan,

Verse 2: And all Naphtali, and the land of Ephraim, and Manasseh, and all the land of Judah, unto the utmost sea,

Verse 3: And the south, and the plain of the valley of Jericho, the city of palm trees, unto Zoar.

Verse 4: And the LORD said unto him, This is the land which I sware unto Abraham, unto Isaac, and unto Jacob, saying, I will give it unto thy seed: I have caused thee to see it with thine eyes, but thou shalt not go over thither.

At this time, Moses died and Joshua took his place. In order to occupy the Canaanite land, Joshua sent two spies to the very prosperous city of Jericho where they found accommodation in the house of a prostitute. As soon as the king became aware of the presence of two spies, he sent some people in search of them but the prostitute misled them and helped the spies escape by night. In return the prostitute asked them to promise her that if they conquer the city, they would not harm her family. Thus, they were the only people who survived and entered among the Jewish people.

Book of Joshua

Chapter 1

Verse 1: Now after the death of Moses the servant of the LORD it came to pass, that the LORD spake unto Joshua the son of Nun, Moses' minister, saying,

Verse 2: Moses my servant is dead; now therefore arise, go over this Jordan, thou, and all this people, unto the land which I do give to them, even to the children of Israel.

Verse 3: Every place that the sole of your foot shall tread upon, that have I given unto you, as I said unto Moses.

Verse 4: From the wilderness and this Lebanon even unto the great river, the river Euphrates, all the land of the Hittites, and unto the great sea toward the going down of the sun, shall be your coast.

In these verses, in the name of the Lord, the command to cross the River Jordan and attack Canaan was given to Joshua. The extent of the Promised Land, which was between Tigris River and Mediterranean Sea, was defined.

Book of Joshua

Chapter 2

Verse 1: And Joshua the son of Nun sent out of Shittim two men to spy secretly, saying, Go view the land, even Jericho. And they went, and came into an harlot's house, named Rahab, and lodged there.

The sixth chapter is concerned with conquering Jericho.

Book of Joshua

Chapter 6

Verse 21: And they utterly destroyed all that was in the city, both man and woman, young and old, and ox, and sheep, and ass, with the edge of the sword.

Verse 22: But Joshua had said unto the two men that had spied out the country, Go into the harlot's house, and bring out thence the woman, and all that she hath, as ye sware unto her.

Verse 23: And the young men that were spies went in, and brought out Rahab, and her father, and her mother, and her brethren, and all that she had; and they brought out all her kindred, and left them without the camp of Israel.

Verse 24: And they burnt the city with fire, and all that was therein: only the silver, and the gold, and the vessels of brass and of iron, they put into the treasury of the house of the LORD.

Verse 25: And Joshua saved Rahab the harlot alive, and her father's household, and all that she had; and she dwelleth in Israel even unto this day; because she hid the messengers, which Joshua sent to spy out Jericho.

Verse 26: And Joshua adjured them at that time, saying, Cursed be the man before the LORD, that riseth up and buildeth this city Jericho: he shall lay the foundation thereof in his firstborn, and in his youngest son shall he set up the gates of it.

Verse 27: So the LORD was with Joshua; and his fame was noised throughout all the country.

In these verses, the brutal massacre, the likes of which had not happened throughout history, is illustrated while it is attributed to their LORD (Yahweh).

Unfortunately, such a holy book, which is considered sacred, and if its orders should be implemented in detail, can establish a very negative and dangerous pattern, which can damage the whole of humanity.

Appreciating crime is worse than committing the crime itself.

In the Old Testament, taking advantage of spies and prostitutes is repeatedly mentioned so that according to this book, it is not only disgraceful and bad; rather it is a divine order.

Destroying the prosperous city of Jericho ("a good-smelling city") -whose name is revealing that it was a beautiful, green, prosperous, and good-smelling city- as well as some other Canaanite cities created enough reason for an old vengeance in Canaanites towards Jews.

A tactical war

The sixth chapter of Joshua's book discusses the way Jericho city - which was a city with a strong fort and castle- was conquered. In these verses, conquering the city is presented as if it was by a miracle that the walls had fallen apart. Unfortunately, lay people do not question what they read and become beguiled by religious clergies who exaggerate the reality for the sake of their own benefit. Reading chapter 8 carefully reveals the way the city was conquered. Jericho was conquered by a war tactic. Chapter 8 of the book of Joshua explains how Joshua ambushed the Ai City at night time with 30,000 warriors. The next day he attacked the city with smaller number of warriors, and pretended to be defeated and escaped. The people of Ai opened the city gates and began to chase them, meanwhile the warriors who had ambushed the city conquered it and surrounded the ones who were outside the castle and massacred them all. In this chapter Joshua openly says that it was a tactic which we used to conquer Jericho.

The book of Joshua

Chapter 8

Verse 5: And I, and all the people that are with me, will approach unto the city: and it shall come to pass, when they come out against us, as at the first, that we will flee before them,

It is clearly obvious that it was not a matter of miracle, or divine help rather a war tactic. Clergies also use their own tactic (making people blind about the reality) and do not tell half of the story. This is called hypocrisy which according to their own ideology must be rejected.

Now it has become abundantly clear that Mandaeans are Canaanites who have hatred towards Jews due to the brutal massacres that they committed. In order to protect their identity and existence, Mandaeans did not give up on their rituals but Jews (like other people throughout the history) followed and imitated other people. One of these instances is the Jew's version of circumcision. When Jews settled in Egypt, they were slaves and subordinate people, and as a result they imitated the superordinate people (Egyptians) in many ways. One of them was to circumcise. On the other hand, the more advanced civilizations like Mandaeans felt no need to follow the other people like Jews in their traditions like circumcision. The result was that after centuries of exhaustion from their own violence and mustiness, a group of Jews along with some other people (Greeks, Romans, and other people of the region like the remaining part of Canaanites) embarked on making a new religion known as Christianity, which was inspired by the advanced ideas of Mandaeism.

Note: By that time, Judaism had been entrenched as a religion and no longer had an ethnic connotation. Also by that time, many Greeks and Romans along with some other people of the region had gathered together around the Old Testament, but the strict instructions of this book had divided the people into two groups.

__The Old Testament was written by the support and funding of Iranian Kings.__

__Who were the Mandaeans?__

Taking into consideration the brief account of Mandaean rituals, traditions, beliefs, and legends which have been provided before, we have somehow been familiar with these people. Now it is time to talk about these people directly. Mandaeans who benefited from having an old civilization were and still are patient and a well tempered people due to having such an old background like any nation which has passed through such a long way, they refrained from war and killing and that is why a group of Jews who were tired of strict and tough rules of Old Testament began to follow this faith.

"Manda" is an Aramaic word which literally means "knowledge" which is exactly equal to the term "gnosis" in Greek and "Erfan/mysticism" in Islam and among Iranians. Mandaeism and Gnosis are considered to be in the same class. Later, these people were also called Sabia. Sabian / صبى / is derived from the word /sab صــب/ which means "pouring water". They are also called Baptist; a tradition that Christians have also borrowed from them, however modern Mandaean prefer to be called "Mandaean Sabian".

The religious traditions of Mandaeans go back to Adam and for them human creation has an older history than that written in the Old Testament. Below are some quotations from the "Tamidiyan" pag 16:

"The Solar Hijri Year 1381-1382 coincides with the year 445372 which is accordingly the birth date of Adam. The origin of calendar among Mandaean Sabian is the birthday of John the Baptist. The solar Hijri year 1381-1382 coincides with 2005 Yahyaay calendar".

It should be noted that John's birth date as mentioned in the New Testament is too close to John the Baptist's birth date. Mandaeans trace back their generation tree to Adam and consider themselves as the successors of Shem, the son of Noah. This means that they are also Semitic and the term anti-Semitism applies more to Mandaean than to Jews. Mandaeans used to settle more in Jerusalem and had some certain rituals due to which they did not get married to other people:

"…What is undoubtedly inferred from Mandaean scriptures and modern Mandaeans' impression from their history is that they used to settle in Palestine and near Jerusalem. According to "Haran Gawaita" which is one of the holy Mandaean scriptures - and contain the history of Mandaeans as well as some predictions about future - Mandaeans used to live in a city where "Jewish rulers" had no way in. Over them was King Ardban (Artabanus) who along with sixty thousand Našoraeans entered the "Median hills" a place where they were free from domination by other folk" (Tamidiyane gharib, p.19).

Note: The Israelites had massacred the Mandaeans brutally. See Torah or five books of Moses for instance chapter 22 and 25 of book of Exodus.

Page 21

"…Taught him Mandaean alphabet when he was 7 years old and when he was 22 years old he was taught "Nathirutha" that is the secret divine knowledge. Yahya Johanna returned to Jerusalem and began to baptize people and revived Mandaean faith. Sixty years after Yahya Johanna, Ruha and Adonay made a plot against Mandaeans and spread Judaism.

There began a battle which led to the death of all Našoraean men. Hibel Ziwa the esteemed angel held a heavenly catastrophe, which destroyed the whole of Jerusalem. By the Lord's will and under the command of Hibel ziwa, uthra Anoš, another divine angel, destroyed all the cities where Jews used to reside and defeated all Jews and darkness by the aid of seven appointees موکل. Then he went to Medai or Median hill and took along with him sixty thousand Našoraeans and Ebhira the son of Shithel who was one of the sons of Artabanus (same as Mandaean Ardban), and appointed him as king.

 If we want to render this religious story to a common language, we might say that after Johanna, the tension between Mandaeans and Jews rose so high that Mandaeans had to migrate to Baghdad and Mesopotamia. It seems that despite the divine massacre of Jews, still migrating to Mesopotamia was a better choice. However, according to this story, Mandaeans built 400 houses or temples in Baghdad, which means that they spread over Baghdad.

These stories continued until the kingdom was no longer held up by King Artabanus' successors. This period coincided with the Sassanid king; Hurdobaian ascending to power. (Sassanid Empire was a great Iranian empire against the Roman Empire.) Nevertheless, there were 170 Mandaean flags left in Baghdad. After this period, there came the Islamic dynasty of "Ishmael", during which there were still 60 Mandaean flags left in Baghdad. Haran Gawaita narrates a story about the contact between a Mandaean called Anoš the son of Dangha with an Arab. According to this narrative, Anoš showed the Arab a book and persuaded him that according to this book they should not harm Našoraeans as they are not allowed to do it. Apparently, this story is indicative of an encounter between Mandaeans and Muslims and the recognition of Mandaeans as the people of the book. To be recognized as the people of the book was the greatest challenge of Mandaeans during the Islamic period.

 Mandaeans is one of the oriental dialects of Aramaic language and had a certain alphabet, which Yahya learnt from Uthra when he was seven years old and was living

hidden in white mountain feeding from tree gum.

<u>Why is there no mention of the Romans in Mandaean books and stories?</u>

Since they were a peaceful people who never looked for power, kingdom and ruling, Romans never had animosity against them, that is why when Jews complained to the king about Jesus they did not pay attention to it until Jews decided to provoke the Romans against Jesus by saying that he had claimed to be the king. When the Romans listened to Jesus Christ, they realized that his intention was not kingdom on earth and realized that he had no danger for Roman kingdom, therefore they set him free. However, the insistence of a group of Jews (the endless animosity of this group was mentioned in previous lines), those who believed in Jesus Christ and his ideas converted to Christianity but those who did not believe in him remained Jewish and they made the Roman commander give Jesus in the Jews' hands and they did with him what has been narrated in New Testament. After that they began to massacre the Mandaeans and forced them to move to south of Iran (Khuzestan) and Iraq.

<u>Final points:</u>

-In order to help coming to conclusion, some points must be mentioned:

-In all areas of the world, the language, traditions, and rituals of neighboring areas are very similar so that in some cases only some small differences distinguish them. These differences are not recognizable for others but just for those people themselves.

-In case of Mandaeans and Jews there are some differences which are in some cases very obvious but in some other cases hard to recognize. For instance in the New Testament, it is mentioned that John wore a leather belt but Mandaeans reject it as they believe that leather is dirty. That is why one cannot understand these delicate points until and unless one has knowledge about Mandaean faith.

-In the case of sacrificing for Jesus Christ, according to Mandaean faith, it is the bird which is recommended, but according to the Old Testament, a bird as a sacrifice is lower in rank than calf and sheep, while in Mandaean faith it is just birds that can be sacrificed.

- According to the Old Testament, Cohein must have been the descendent of Levites, so if Yahya (as a high deity) was Jewish, he should have been the descendent of Levites, and as a result, his generation tree and his father's (Zacharya) generation tree should have been clear. On the same basis, Jesus Christ's mother, Mary, should have been the descendent of Levites and should have had a clear generation tree. However, since this is not the case, John/Yahja could not have been a Jew and since he was a relative of Mary and Jesus Christ, therefore they were not Jew either, rather they were Mandaean (Canaanite.) On the other hand the opposite is practiced in the case of Yahya who had different habits and rituals. Rather than accepting him, Yahya is considered as a great danger and is condemned to death.

Consequently, all these cases held true in the case of John's relatives including Jesus Christ, and at the end the Jews succeeded in killing him because according to Coheins' dream and the interpretation made by the greatest dream interpreter, John was a danger to Jews and Judaism - but John left that mission to Jesus Christ. Taking into consideration what we have mentioned earlier about the way Jews handled their messengers and prophets, it can be argued that if John was a Jew, then they would not have embarked on killing him.

Final points and concluding remarks

The narratives gathered in the New Testament have been written through several years and by various people, which makes it contradictory and heterogeneous. That is why one cannot draw any kind of a clear and specific instructions or plan in any regard.

Those Romans who converted to Judaism wrote most of the contents of the New Testament (even Gospels). These Romans who were under the influence of Greek culture, had no profound knowledge of Jews/Arabs (nomads), and the knowledge that they had acquired was more through word of mouth or what they had read in the Old Testament. Consequently, they had no knowledge about real Jews (nomad Arab), their traditions, rituals or other big and small cultural points, nor any knowledge about this religion or ethnic or folk knowledge about Jews. As a result, there are remarkable differences between their stories. In particular, one of the main weak points of the Romans who had come after Greeks was to forget the Mandaean (Canaanite) stories because most of them had not seen these people. That is why these issues were not developed in their writings. Despite it, they were not able to ignore the story of John or other points while they themselves were not aware of the Mandaean roots of those stories.

<u>Finally: even if one can prove that Jesus Christ and his mother were Jews, still there is no need for Christians to feel themselves in debt to Jews so that they embark on establishing Zionist churches. Most of the predecessors of Mohammad were pagan but neither Mohammad supported it nor any of his heir defended paganism. They did not feel themselves in its debt, and even worse, obliged to publish pagans' texts along with the Quran.</u>

May 2014   Uppsala - Sweden

M. Hassan Baygan

hassan@baygan.net

hassan@baygan.org

www.baygan.org

http://www.readbookonline.net/read/16632/42788/
(book of Joshua)
http://www.catholic.org/bible/book.php?id=2 (book of exodus)
http://www.readbibleonline.net/?page_id=9 (book of exodus)
http://www.readbookonline.net/title/8847/ (book of numbers)
http://www.readbookonline.net/title/16631/ (book of Deuteronomy)

My Philosophy, Method and Followers

Socrates

I am like my mother; I give birth to all others, but have no child of my own (philosophy!)

Hassan Baygan:

I have a complete, logical, rational, precise, solid, independent child (philosophy) which is designed for the present and the future of humans. A philosophy which isn't like a continuous chain, but more like circles who's rings are all connected to each other.

Buddha:

I do not fight because, in a combat, the side that is defeated becomes heart broken, disgusted and sad.

Hassan Baygan:

Life is full of open and hidden struggles. Even a sporting competition which is played for fun can result in someone's regret and sorrow. One must look at the real life and view the struggle as an inevitable part of it. But we can not only look after our own benefits and use inhuman ways to win at all costs and damage to others. On the contrary, we must transform these struggles into a common fight to achieve a peaceful and beneficial life for all.

Mohammad the Muslim's prophet:

To establish his beliefs Mohammad reached for a sword and as the result many were killed.

Hassan Baygan:

To prove my ideas, I will never resort to violence, in deed or in words, and I'm absolutely opposed to shedding of any blood. Anyone who is willing to follow my philosophy must be the same, otherwise she/he will not be my follower. But everyone has the right to defend themselves, especially when it comes to their lives!

Explanation of the Universe:

Our knowledge is still very limited, we have reached such a level that we must definitely declare that we still do not know the universe, where we came from and where we are heading?

The followers of my philosophy must:

-Use scientific and logical knowledge and analysis.

-Whenever and wherever they discover a mistake, acknowledge that without any hesitation and endeavor to correct it!

-They shall, during my life and thereafter, refrain from using force, lies, deceit and sophistry, or unbalanced and illogical arguments, to prove any parts of my thought and philosophy.

-They must be kind and brave!

-Base all their work on the foundation of real science and firm logic.

The one and only eternal law:

Everything is subject to change!

There were never any laws that could cover all of the earth's habitants now or in the future. All laws must be changed and improved upon in relations to time and location. That is the only ongoing law!

I am an ordinary person and my behavior is affected by time and place. Whatever that I have done or am doing now, is not necessarily correct and universal; and whatever I haven't done or don't today, is not necessarily wrong. Therefore, my personal life and traits must not become a sample or role for others to follow! One must always refer to Change as <u>"The only eternal law."</u>

Mars 2018
Uppsala – Sweden

M. Hassan Baygan

<u>www.baygan.org</u>

Hassan Baygan